# GOGI Group Certifi
# YOUR PROOF OF COUR

*Today's*

MW01102639

*Dear Student,*

*Before you turn in this completed course book, please fill out this PROOF OF PROGRAM COMPLETION and get it signed and dated. Once completed, gently tear out this page and keep it for your records. This will be your documentation that you have done your part. Having your proof of course completion signed and in your possession may come in handy if something happens and your completion is not recorded in your corrections file.*

**DO NOT SEND THIS SHEET IN FOR CREDIT. TURN YOUR WORKBOOK IN AND KEEP THIS SHEET.**

## ME

My last name:_____ My first name: _____

My ID number:_____ My housing: _____

The name of the institution where I turned in my completed work:

_____

My Group was completed *(circle one)*

in housing     in classroom   in gym     in dayroom     (NO solo study allowed)

Date I started this course: _____

Date I completed this course: _____

**KEEP THIS PAGE – TURN IN YOUR WORKBOOK**

## PEER

The name of my Peer Mentor (or have your cellie or friend) who witnessed me

doing my coursework: _____
<br>print clearly

Their ID number:_____Housing: _____

Peer sign here:_____Date: _____

**KEEP THIS PAGE – TURN IN YOUR WORKBOOK**

## STAFF

The staff or GOGI representative who received my work is:

_____
<br>print clearly

Staff or GOGI representative who received this workbook please sign here:

_____Date: _____

**KEEP THIS PAGE – TURN IN YOUR WORKBOOK**

# GOGI Group Certificate Course

Published by: GOGI Education
A division of Getting Out by Going In (GOGI)

---

**Please do not make copies of this book.**
**GOGI needs these composition books to be purchased.**

Making copies of this book is dishonest, and does not help GOGI expand and grow to serve all prisoners. GOGI offers many free materials and services, however if copies of this composition book are made we cannot sustain ourselves and fewer people will have access to GOGI.

*Please check our website for donor-assistance, multiple discounts, and bulk order pricing of this and all GOGI certificate programs.*

---

GOGI EDU is a division of the nonprofit, Getting Out by Going In (GOGI)

ISBN: 978-0-9972875-6-1

First edition, March 2016
Second edition, May 2017
Third edition, April 2018

Typesetting and design: Candace Webster

*This book is another in the family of GOGI materials such as:*
*Workshops, DVDs, curricula, educational media, and self-study materials designed to promote the GOGI Culture, and teach the GOGI TOOLS FOR POSITIVE DECISION-MAKING.*

# GET READY FOR

# GOGI

# ORIENTATION

## Start every cycle with the ORIENTATION WEEK Meeting in 3 easy Steps

1. Be certain to sign in every day in the gray area at the top of each page

2. Read the **GOGI ORIENTATION INFORMATION**

3. Enjoy your **GOGI Meeting**

# WARNING!

## If you want GOGI credit for this course, make certain you read the requirements below.
### DO NOT start this course unless you meet the requirements below

# Requirements for the GOGI Group Certificate Program
### aka: *The GOGI Spider Table Course*

1) **GOGI CREDIT** – If you complete every page of this course on your own time, documenting your GOGI group work, then it is likely GOGI will issue credit for this course in the form of a GOGI CERTIFICATE and you will also have a GOGI REPORT CARD that documents this and any other GOGI courses you complete. GOGI credit is different than credit you may receive from your prison.

2) **NO TIME OFF** – It is very likely that you will not earn time off your sentence for completion of this course. It is probable you will receive a form of credit, but this credit will not likely result in time off. If receiving time off is a determining factor in your level of interest in this course, please assume you will receive only the credit GOGI offers and that is determined by what is permitted by the institution. Please do not start this course if you are doing it for time off or to go home early. That is probably not going to happen with this course and it will most likely frustrate you. You may earn a certificate from GOGI – if staff requests a certificate from GOGI – but this course probably will not result in a reduction of time.

3) **NO SOLO** – This is a group course, this is not a solo course. You will complete this course on your own time outside of your group meetings and this is how you earn GOGI credit, by documenting your meetings. While GOGI has solo-study courses available at many institutions, this course is specifically and exclusively a *GOGI Group course* and permits you to document your group meetings on your own time for GOGI credit. As such, credit will not be given to anyone doing this course as a solo study.

4) **GROUP SIZE** – A GOGI Group is defined as having no fewer than two and no more than twelve members. This means if you are permitted to do GOGI as an "in cell" course, you may do this course with your cellie, or you may even be able to meet for fifteen weekly meetings with a friend during your day room time. As long as you document weekly meetings for fifteen weeks and as long as you complete each question, your work will qualify to be processed for GOGI credit (remember this is different than prison credit.)

5) **NAMING YOUR GROUP** – To help our team of volunteers and to help us remain organized, all GOGI Groups are identified by a team nickname with group member names clearly documented each week. The group name and the group members names should be clearly written on the required spaces where the group name and group members names are required. Team names like "GOGI 4 Lifers" and "GOGI Rising" are sufficient. Even something like "GOGI B yard 1 Block Dayroom" or "Cell 234 GOGI" are good.

6) **CALENDAR** – GOGI meetings are held according to the GOGI Calendar. This means that you will only have the meeting based on the tool that all other GOGI groups are studying that week. If it is the first week of January then all of GOGI is going to be working on BOSS OF MY BRAIN. If it is the last week of December then all of GOGI is working on ULTIMATE FREEDOM. Your credit is earned by holding fifteen weekly meetings ACCORDING TO THE CALENDAR. If you miss a week you will miss a tool. That is OK. STAY ON CALENDAR.

7) **WEEKLY MEETINGS** – Each week you will follow the GOGI MEETING FORMAT outlined in this and all other GOGI materials. Meetings are sometimes 15 minutes but often last 2 hours. As long as you follow the official meeting format with 2-12 participants then you are on track.

8) **DATE YOUR PAGES** – Credit is only provided when you follow the instructions which includes dating and signing at the top of every page. At the top of each meeting page you are to write down the month (examples are January, February, March), the day (examples are Monday Tuesday, Wednesday) the date (examples are the 3rd, 4th, 5th) and the year (examples are 2019, 2020, 2021). If you do not date your pages your course is automatically disqualified for credit.

9) **FIFTEEN WEEKLY MEETINGS** – This course is considered acceptable for review of credit only after FIFTEEN WEEKLY MEETINGS have been held according to MEETING FORMAT and the GOGI STUDY CALENDAR and those meetings are documented on the appropriate pages in this workbook. GOGI is a calendar-based organization, not a tool-based organization. Fifteen weekly meetings qualifies for completion review.

10) **REMEMBER - STAY ON CALENDAR** – Remain on calendar. If you are on lockdown one week, then you will not study one of the tools. You will REMAIN ON CALENDAR, skip that tool and remain united with the rest of the GOGI Nation in our universal study schedule.

11) **REPEAT, REPEAT, REPEAT** – You are permitted by GOGI to earn a GOGI certificate for completion of this course THREE TIMES EACH YEAR! That is correct. You can earn THREE GOGI certificates by completing this course three times each year. Why can you repeat this course? Because we want you engaged in GOGI Group study as an on-going way for you to associate with people who want to go home and become the solution in their communities. Completion of a GOGI Group cycle every four months is deserving of a GOGI credit.

12) **COMPLETED WORKBOOKS** – Do not mail this workbook into GOGI's mailroom. Do not mail in the PROOF OF COMPLETION sheet into GOGI's mailroom. This workbook is exclusively for the processing at the institutional level. GOGI will not process these courses as they are designed specifically for institutional use. They were designed to help institutions meet the growing need for more and more GOGI studies. Our mailroom volunteers cannot and will not process these courses. They must be processed at your institution. Please ask other GOGI students or ask the office at your institution how you are advised to receive credit for your completed work.

*WHEW!!!! We are glad THAT is over!*
*Now, if you are willing to complete this course accepting*
*all of the above, then...Complete the information on the next*
*page and let's get your GOGI On!*

# GOGI GROUP CERTIFICATE COURSE

Note to students: At the end of your fifteen meetings (which will take fifteen weeks or more), please turn this packet into your group facilitator at your institution. Your staff will be working with GOGI to issue credit for your completion. This coursebook may be returned to you once credit is issued. This coursebook may serve as the necessary documentation of completion if institution records are not available. Your completed coursework will also come in handy as you mentor others.

Date I began this course: _____

Date I completed 15 meetings: _____

## This GOGI GROUP CERTIFICATE COURSEBOOK belongs to:

Last Name: _____ First Name: _____

ID Number: _____ Housing: _____

Institution Name: _____

Mailing address: _____

City:_____ State: _____ Zip Code: _____

**↓ DON'T FORGET TO FILL THIS OUT ↓**

## Details About my GOGI GROUP:

The day of the week my GOGI Study Group meets is: _____

The place my GOGI Study Group meets is: _____

The time of day my GOGI Study Group meets is: _____

The staff sponsor or staff facilitator for my group is: _____

**↑ DON'T FORGET TO FILL THIS OUT ↑**

This course book is called the "Spider Table Course" because the GOGI leaders on D Yard at High Desert State Prison in Susanville, California gave this course that nickname. At High Desert they do GOGI in their housing units with guys gathered around the metal "spider" tables in the dayroom. Hence, the nickname Spider-Table Course. This course is intended to support small group study. Small group study is highly encouraged by GOGI. We want you to take GOGI home!

**DAILY SIGN-IN – GROUP CERTIFICATE COURSE**
**If you want to receive credit, please fill out the information below:**

The month is_____ The day of the month is _____ The year is_____ Signature _____
Meeting location_____ Start time _____ Number of people in my Group _____
**MY GROUP STUDIES ACCORDING TO THE GOGI CALENDAR (circle one)   YES   NO**

**SIGN-IN**
**Remember to SIGN-IN every day!**
**Sign-in every day to document your participation and study.**
**This record is your proof of participation.**

# GOGI GROUP
# CERTIFICATE COURSE

1) FIFTEEN - Each GOGI Group cycle requires FIFTEEN MEETINGS with all group members.

2) CERTIFICATES - Once you have completed FIFTEEN MEETINGS as a group, your group members have earned a CERTIFICATE OF COMPLETION from GOGI. This will need to be ordered by supervising staff by submission of an electronic excel spreadsheet order form submitted to GOGI. We will provide your staff with this form. If you are not getting an official GOGI certificate with the GOGI logo and GOGI signatures... ask for one! We want you in our data base and getting the data from your facility helps us support you in your GOGI journey.

3) NO SOLO - It is not possible to complete any of the study without a weekly grour meeting. If you are on lock down, you will pick right back up on calendar when you can meet again.

4) In-cell - This course is In-cell study and requires you to do significant writing and reading and practice beyond your weekly meeting. This is why you may receive credit for your weekly meetings from your institution AND credit from GOGI for completion of this workbook. On the other hand, you may ONLY receive credit for completion of the workbook. The point is, GOGI only documents your in-cell completion of your workbook, as this is what is needed to advance in GOGI.

# How Goofy is

When you live life with the GOGI Tools to guide you, life can be a lot of fun. Students of GOGI have fun. Learning is fun, especially when you learn The GOGI Way!

# Your GOGI?

**DAILY SIGN-IN – GROUP CERTIFICATE COURSE**
If you want to receive credit, please fill out the information below:

The month is_____ The day of the month is _____ The year is_____ Signature _____
Meeting location_____ Start time _____ Number of people in my Group _____
MY GROUP STUDIES ACCORDING TO THE GOGI CALENDAR (circle one)    YES    NO

# DO YOU KNOW YOUR GOGI?

You know your GOGI if you can answer the following questions. These questions are provided to GOGI by students contacting GOGI after their successful Board hearings. They state the Board asked these questions during their interviews.

- **What are the four sections GOGI TOOLS?**

  1) TOOLS OF THE BODY          3) TOOLS OF MOVING FORWARD

  2) TOOLS OF CHOICE            4) TOOLS OF CREATION

- **What are the names of the GOGI Tools?**

  BOSS OF MY BRAIN, BELLY BREATHING, FIVE SECOND LIGHTSWITCH,
  POSITIVE THOUGHTS, POSITIVE WORDS, POSITIVE ACTIONS,
  CLAIM RESPONSIBILITY, LET GO, FOR–GIVE,
  WHAT IF, REALITY CHECK, ULTIMATE FREEDOM

- **Who created the GOGI Tools and who created GOGI?**

  Prisoners created the GOGI Tools to share with other prisoners. All GOGI materials were given to GOGI by prisoners.

- **What is the GOGI Pledge and who created it?**

  A group of prisoners created the GOGI Pledge to unite all students learning GOGI so together they could make their communities better places to live.

  *May our commitment (repeat)*
  *To the study of GOGI (repeat)*
  *Grant us the joy (repeat)*
  *Of giving and receiving (repeat)*
  *So that our inner freedom (repeat)*
  *May be of maximum service (repeat)*
  *To those we love (repeat)*
  *And infinite others (repeat)*

- **Why does GOGI have a calendar?**

  GOGI students study according to the GOGI Calendar because when all of GOGI studies according to the GOGI Calendar, no person will ever be alone in their GOGI studies. Each week of the year we focus on a different GOGI Tool.

## DAILY SIGN-IN – GROUP CERTIFICATE COURSE
### If you want to receive credit, please fill out the information below:

The month is_____ The day of the month is _____ The year is_____ Signature _____

Meeting location_____ Start time _____ Number of people in my Group _____

**MY GROUP STUDIES ACCORDING TO THE GOGI CALENDAR (circle one)    YES    NO**

- ## Why is GOGI Group study coordinated with the calendar?
  So all students of GOGI everywhere are united in the study of our tools.

- ## Who Created GOGI's Official Meeting Format and Why?
  Prisoners with experience in many different types of group meetings created the official meeting format. It is used so all GOGI meetings follow a uniform format that is familiar to anyone attending meetings in different locations.

- ## What are the Keywords each of the TOOLS?

### TOOLS OF THE BODY
**BOSS OF MY BRAIN:** THE THREE PARTS: There are three parts that matter: SMART PART, EMOTIONAL PART, and the OLD HABIT PART. Which one is the boss right now?

**BELLY BREATHING:** ONE HAND ON MY CHEST, ONE HAND ON MY BELLY. WHICH ONE IS MOVING RIGHT NOW? My brain works better when my belly moves.

**FIVE SECOND LIGHTSWITCH:** OLD THOUGHT → NEW ACTION. I have an OLD THOUGHT and I have a NEW ACTION.

### TOOLS OF CHOICE
**POSITIVE THOUGHTS:** Is it Powerful? Productive? Positive?

**POSITIVE WORDS:** Is it Powerful? Productive? Positive?

**POSITIVE ACTIONS:** Is it Powerful? Productive? Positive?

### TOOLS OF MOVING FORWARD
**CLAIM RESPONSIBILITY:** AM I PROUD OF THIS CHOICE? I am responsible for all my actions and all my reactions today.

**LET GO:** HAND/SQUASH/TOSS. When bothered, I put the feeling in my hand, squash it, and toss it away from me.

**FOR–GIVE:** FOR ME TO GIVE, I NEED DISTANCE FROM HARM. For me to give, I unhook from the past, and find my internal freedom.

### TOOLS OF CREATION
**WHAT IF:** WHAT IF I AM NOT MY PAST? No to the past = yes to the future.

**REALITY CHECK:** TEN AND TWO RULE. Ten steps forward and two steps back is still eight steps ahead.

**ULTIMATE FREEDOM:** BEING FREE IS UP TO ME. Living a life of service gives me ULTIMATE FREEDOM.

**DAILY SIGN-IN – GROUP CERTIFICATE COURSE**
**If you want to receive credit, please fill out the information below:**

The month is_____ The day of the month is _____ The year is_____ Signature _____

Meeting location_____ Start time _____ Number of people in my Group _____

**MY GROUP STUDIES ACCORDING TO THE GOGI CALENDAR (circle one)     YES     NO**

# Foreword

## By Coach Taylor, Lead Volunteer

The GOGI Group has always been the foundation of all GOGI studies. From the very first group that sat on the floor of the gym/chapel on Wednesdays at FCI Terminal Island, California, to the groups in prisons all over the world right now, the GOGI Group is what distinguishes GOGI as more of a 'culture' than a 'program'.

A culture is something you become A PART OF while a program is something that you DO. At GOGI, we ARE GOGI, we don't DO GOGI. Our small groups of two to twelve individuals are powerful because we change the culture. We support our group members while strengthening our own ability to move through the world with powerful and positive decision-making tools.

I am still amazed when I travel across the United States and I hear groups of GOGI students recite our pledge. I am amazed when I walk by a GOGI study group and I hear otherwise quiet and reserved individuals contributing to the group in powerful and thoughtful ways. I am amazed when I hear of prisoners getting out and continuing to live The GOGI Way.

I remember the day I realized that GOGI was bigger than anything I could have possibly imagined. I was going from one SHU cell to the next visiting prisoners in a Maximum Security housing unit at California Correctional Institution in Tehachapi, California. There were men in those eight-foot cells who had been locked away for 20-30 years, without any contact with anyone outside of those who came into the housing unit to work. The moment I KNEW that GOGI would be on this earth for 300+ years was when I approached a cell and the man was standing on his bunk. He was reaching toward his air vent with his words. I looked and then I listened. He was speaking to his neighbor about GOGI.

"Are you talking GOGI?" I asked him.

"Yeah, we're having a GOGI meeting," the prisoner replied.

Through the air vents these two men held their weekly GOGI meetings.

Later that month when I went to Pelican Bay State Prison SHU housing unit in California, I walked from pod to pod and received the paperwork of men who were holding GOGI meetings through the bars. While in a maximum security setting and never being let out of their cell except one at a time, these men held their weekly

## DAILY SIGN-IN – GROUP CERTIFICATE COURSE
### If you want to receive credit, please fill out the information below:

The month is_____ The day of the month is _____The year is_____ Signature _____

Meeting location_____ Start time _____ Number of people in my Group _____

**MY GROUP STUDIES ACCORDING TO THE GOGI CALENDAR (circle one)    YES    NO**

groups. When the laws changed and these men were moved to General Population yards, it was feared that they would return to the criminal ways that got them locked away from humanity. Instead, the men who had studied GOGI every day for two years were transferred to yards where other prisoners began to join their small GOGI Groups. These "hardened criminals" were evolving as the most powerful leaders for a positive culture shift on the yards where they were transferred.

There was the time I was asked if I would come speak to a group of prisoners in another state. They had no time permitted to program and the administration had no interest in GOGI so they identified a graveyard officer who had read and supported the GOGI studies. During the graveyard shift he would permit the Men of GOGI to leave their bunks and hold their meeting – in the middle of the night. When I arrived at the jail on a snowy and dark night, I could not believe the determination of these men who would not be stopped by administrative resistance to their new culture. When I walked into that room, nearly 100 prisoners stood up and recited the GOGI Pledge by heart.

I have watched GOGI grow from a tiny group of curious men sitting in a circle on the floor at Terminal Island to a massive movement that is returning incarcerated people back to their families and communities. They return not as a problem – but as the SOLUTION: armed only with their GOGI Tools.

My hope is that you experience GOGI for more than just the "program" to which you are now enrolled. My hope is that you truly see the movement GOGI creates as a new and more positive culture which emerges out of the darkest and most desperate places on earth. My hope is that these tools, which were created by and for prisoners, become part of you and help you become all you hope to be.

As our GOGI students frequently say...

I am GOGI-4-Life! (And that is one life sentence you will never mind having.)


With Love,

Coach Taylor,
Lead Volunteer

The Faces o GOG Graduate

Your Face Belongs Here!

## DAILY SIGN-IN – GROUP CERTIFICATE COURSE
**If you want to receive credit, please fill out the information below:**

The month is_____ The day of the month is _____The year is_____ Signature _____
Meeting location_____ Start time _____ Number of people in my Group _____
**MY GROUP STUDIES ACCORDING TO THE GOGI CALENDAR (circle one)    YES     NO**

**SIGN-IN**
**Remember to SIGN-IN every day!**
**Sign-in every day to document your participation and study.**
**This record is your proof of participation.**

# READY? SET? LET'S GOGI!

In groups of two to twelve members (if you have thirteen or more, break into smaller subgroups) have volunteers this orientation section.

---

YOUR GOGI GROUP NAME
Much like sports teams or civic organizations, having a group name will help encourage a positive, prosocial team effort for your group. Your name could be as simple as "prison, yard, year" so as an example, your name could be the Pelican A Yard 2017 GOGI Group. Once your group decides on a name, write it below:

*MY GROUP NAME IS:* _____

---

# GOGI is Calendar-Based Study *(volunteers to read aloud)*

*(volunteer)* Unlike many other "programs," GOGI does not study according to a linear progression of concepts or steps. GOGI is a calendar-based organization. For the next fifteen weeks you will study according to the GOGI Calendar.

*(volunteer)* This means that if your group is unable to hold a GOGI Group meeting during any particular week, you will skip the tool that week. That is fine. It is more important for you to remain on the GOGI Calendar.

*(volunteer)* GOGI is a community of individuals who make their daily decisions with the help of their GOGI Tools. All GOGI students study according to the GOGI Calendar. If you follow the GOGI Calendar you will never, ever be alone in your GOGI study. We want you to be part of a growing community of like-minded members who are united in their commitment to make more positive decisions, regardless of the enormous obstacles that may seem to be in the way.

*(volunteer)* Your group will meet fifteen times for you to complete this course and earn recognition for your participation. You may study some tools more than once. You may not study a particular tool at all. That is fine, as long as you study according to the GOGI Calendar.

# Remember, ALWAYS remain on calendar.

## DAILY SIGN-IN – GROUP CERTIFICATE COURSE
**If you want to receive credit, please fill out the information below:**

The month is_____ The day of the month is _____ The year is_____ Signature _____

Meeting location_____ Start time _____ Number of people in my Group _____

**MY GROUP STUDIES ACCORDING TO THE GOGI CALENDAR (circle one)    YES    NO**

*(volunteer)* Each week GOGI students study one tool based on the calendar. (Identify this week's Tool by using the The GOGI Calendar below.)

# The GOGI Study Calendar
*GOGI weeks always start on Monday.*
*Each month will start on Monday 1st, 2nd, 3rd, 4th, 5th, 6th, or 7th.*

### JANUARY
Week 1 BOSS OF MY BRAIN
Week 2 BELLY BREATHING
Week 3 FIVE SECOND LIGHTSWITCH
Week 4 POSITIVE THOUGHTS
Week 5 REVIEW ABOVE

### FEBRUARY
Week 1 POSITIVE WORDS
Week 2 POSITIVE ACTIONS
Week 3 CLAIM RESPONSIBILITY
Week 4 LET GO
Week 5 REVIEW ABOVE

### MARCH
Week 1 FOR–GIVE
Week 2 WHAT IF
Week 3 REALITY CHECK
Week 4 ULTIMATE FREEDOM
Week 5 REVIEW ABOVE

### APRIL
Week 1 BOSS OF MY BRAIN
Week 2 BELLY BREATHING
Week 3 FIVE SECOND LIGHTSWITCH
Week 4 POSITIVE THOUGHTS
Week 5 REVIEW ABOVE

### MAY
Week 1 POSITIVE WORDS
Week 2 POSITIVE ACTIONS
Week 3 CLAIM RESPONSIBILITY
Week 4 LET GO
Week 5 REVIEW ABOVE

### JUNE
Week 1 FOR–GIVE
Week 2 WHAT IF
Week 3 REALITY CHECK
Week 4 ULTIMATE FREEDOM
Week 5 REVIEW ABOVE

### JULY
Week 1 BOSS OF MY BRAIN
Week 2 BELLY BREATHING
Week 3 FIVE SECOND LIGHTSWITCH
Week 4 POSITIVE THOUGHTS
Week 5 REVIEW ABOVE

### AUGUST
Week 1 POSITIVE WORDS
Week 2 POSITIVE ACTIONS
Week 3 CLAIM RESPONSIBILITY
Week 4 LET GO
Week 5 REVIEW ABOVE

### SEPTEMBER
Week 1 FOR–GIVE
Week 2 WHAT IF
Week 3 REALITY CHECK
Week 4 ULTIMATE FREEDOM
Week 5 REVIEW ABOVE

### OCTOBER
Week 1 BOSS OF MY BRAIN
Week 2 BELLY BREATHING
Week 3 FIVE SECOND LIGHTSWITCH
Week 4 POSITIVE THOUGHTS
Week 5 REVIEW ABOVE

### NOVEMBER
Week 1 POSITIVE WORDS
Week 2 POSITIVE ACTIONS
Week 3 CLAIM RESPONSIBILITY
Week 4 LET GO
Week 5 REVIEW ABOVE

### DECEMBER
Week 1 FOR–GIVE
Week 2 WHAT IF
Week 3 REALITY CHECK
Week 4 ULTIMATE FREEDOM
Week 5 REVIEW ABOVE

## DAILY SIGN-IN – GROUP CERTIFICATE COURSE
**If you want to receive credit, please fill out the information below:**

The month is_____ The day of the month is _____ The year is_____ Signature _____
Meeting location_____ Start time _____ Number of people in my Group _____
**MY GROUP STUDIES ACCORDING TO THE GOGI CALENDAR (circle one)     YES     NO**

# The GOGI Tools *(volunteers read aloud)*

*(volunteer)* Before you get started with Week One of THE GOGI GROUP CERTIFICATE COURSE, take some time to read the following pages which are a brief introduction to the GOGI TOOLS FOR POSITIVE DECISION-MAKING.

## The Tools are broken into four sections:

### TOOLS OF THE BODY
- BOSS OF MY BRAIN
- BELLY BREATHING
- FIVE SECOND LIGHTSWITCH

### TOOLS OF CHOICE
- POSITIVE THOUGHTS
- POSITIVE WORDS
- POSITIVE ACTIONS

### TOOLS OF MOVING FORWARD
- CLAIM RESPONSIBILITY
- LET GO
- FOR–GIVE

### TOOLS OF CREATION
- WHAT IF
- REALITY CHECK
- ULTIMATE FREEDOM

### Understanding the GOGI Tools *(volunteer)*
Each tool has KEYWORDS, a STATEMENT OF PURPOSE AND OWNERSHIP, an OBJECTIVE, a TOOL INTRO, and tips on HOW TO USE the tool. These sections will help you to understand the basics of the GOGI Tools.

### The GOGI Calendar *(volunteer)*
Around the globe, no matter where you are, when you study according to the GOGI Calendar, you will never be alone in your GOGI studies. It is MORE IMPORTANT to be on the Calendar than to start GOGI studies with a particular tool.

## THE BASIC GOGI STUDY GROUP RULES

*Have volunteers read the rules below. All members then need to write their initials on the line to the left of each paragraph, signing that you understand what is expected of you.* **MAKE SURE YOU READ AND INITIAL EACH NUMBERED ITEM BELOW.**

INITIAL HERE ____
**1. I understand that all GOGI meetings are based on the THE GOGI STUDY CALENDAR. If a meeting is missed, we do not 'make-up' that tool. We stay on calendar.**

INITIAL HERE ____
2. I understand that all GOGI Groups assemble in a circle of 2 to 12 members. To the best of my ability, I will assist in setting up and returning the room to as clean or cleaner than when it was offered as a place to meet.

INITIAL HERE ____
3. I understand that even if there are a hundred people in the room who are in GOGI, my GOGI Group has no more than twelve people. Group size is an important component in GOGI. I realize there may be multiple small circles in a room and I will respect the noise level and not become distracting to other groups.

INITIAL HERE ____
4. I understand I must attend all twelve to fifteen GOGI meetings to qualify as having completed one GOGI program cycle.

INITIAL HERE ____
5. I understand this coursebook should be filled out during or after each meeting.

INITIAL HERE ____
6. I understand that in no way should anyone ever need to pay anything or do any favors to be a part of GOGI.

INITIAL HERE ____
7. I understand that this packet may be provided to me by the institution, and if so, the institution will acknowledge me for my work in this course. I understand my completion will be documented by the institution in collaboration with GOGI.

INITIAL HERE ____
8. I understand that the most effective GOGI study is when each student is provided at least one GOGI book that becomes their personal property and it is my responsibility to continue to study GOGI after course completion.

All of life is based on a delicate balance. Cause and effect are the scales with which this balance is maintained. If you want the scales to tip in your favor, you must be willing to invest more, do more, and be more. This is how we tip the scales to our favor. Following the rules and creating discipline in our life is an essential tool for tipping those scales. Embrace and respect your 'rules' as they are the path to your freedom.

Coach Taylor, Lead Volunteer

# BIG GROUPS & SMALL GROUPS

*(volunteer to read)* If your institution is able, you might be doing GOGI in a gym with 100 or more other GOGI students.  That would be called your LARGER GROUP.  But every LARGER GROUP also has SMALL STUDY GROUPS. In a room of 100 GOGI students you would see about 10 SMALL STUDY GROUPS formed in small circles for their study. If you have more than twelve members, you need to divide into an additional SMALL STUDY GROUP.

# GROUP MEMBERS

*(volunteer to read)* It is best if your smaller study groups can be formed by housing units. This way study can occur among individuals who live near each other, and when on modified lockdowns GOGI study is more likely to continue if members are in the same housing units.

# GROUP NAME

*(volunteer to read)* Below is art created by The GOGI Group Phoenix of KVSP. The group voted on their name and created a logo.

## DAILY SIGN-IN – GROUP CERTIFICATE COURSE
**If you want to receive credit, please fill out the information below:**

The month is_____ The day of the month is _____The year is_____ Signature _____
Meeting location_____ Start time _____ Number of people in my Group _____
**MY GROUP STUDIES ACCORDING TO THE GOGI CALENDAR (circle one)   YES   NO**

*My name is:* _____

*MY GROUP MEMBERS ARE: (It is easiest if you pass the books around and let each member print their name.)*

2. _____

3. _____

4. _____

5. _____

6. _____

7. _____

8. _____

9. _____

10. _____

11. _____

12. _____

*If there are more than twelve people, break into two smaller groups.*

*MY GROUP MEETING DETAILS:*

*My small group name is:* _____

*The day of the week my group meets is:* _____

*The time of day is:* _____

*Our meetings started on this date:* _____

*Our projected completion date is set for:* _____

*Our group will be learning according to the GOGI Calendar:* _____ yes _____ no

*Our group has a staff sponsor or staff facilitator:* _____ yes _____ no

*Their name is:* _____

*(By the end of the course, it is requested that you say "Thank you" to your staff sponsor or staff facilitator. Oftentimes, the staff assisting GOGI Groups puts in many more hours than you may think in their effort to support the group. Sometimes they are ridiculed for their support of prisoners and programming. Sometimes they are behind in other work and this is truly a burden. Sometimes sitting in on GOGI Groups takes them away from family and friends. Please be mindful of their sacrifice and voice a "Thank you" at some point during your course.)*

**DAILY SIGN-IN – GROUP CERTIFICATE COURSE**
**If you want to receive credit, please fill out the information below:**

The month is_____ The day of the month is _____ The year is_____ Signature _____

Meeting location_____ Start time _____ Number of people in my Group _____

**MY GROUP STUDIES ACCORDING TO THE GOGI CALENDAR (circle one)     YES     NO**

## YOUR GOGI STUDY GROUP RULES

*(volunteer to read)* In addition to the basic rules set by GOGI, your study group will need its own group rules. During your orientation meeting, please meet with your group and write the unique group rules to which all members agree. Some popular examples are: No cross talking, no talking for longer than two minutes, what is said in our meeting remains in our meeting, and if you miss two meetings you forfeit your seat. What are your group rules?

Your GROUP RULES HERE: *(Group to propose and agree on ten rules.)*

1. _____

2. _____

3. _____

4. _____

5. _____

6. _____

7. _____

8. _____

9. _____

10. _____

## MEETING LENGTH

*(volunteer to read)* The GOGI students state that the optimal time for a GOGI meeting is two hours. However, the average meeting length is 90 minutes. There are times when a very short meeting is necessary. A short meeting is better than no meeting.

## GOGI LEADERS

*(volunteer to read)* The finest GOGI leader is the leader who does not speak much and they sit with their group, they do not stand over their group. The GOGI leader should inspire an even distribution of dialog among all members. Please be mindful that everyone is encouraged to speak and the group may wish to assign someone to raise their hand when anyone is talking too long. Your GOGI Group leader is a good leader when they let group members do the talking and they sit in support.

## DAILY SIGN-IN – GROUP CERTIFICATE COURSE
**If you want to receive credit, please fill out the information below:**

The month is_____ The day of the month is _____ The year is_____ Signature _____

Meeting location_____ Start time _____ Number of people in my Group _____

**MY GROUP STUDIES ACCORDING TO THE GOGI CALENDAR (circle one)    YES    NO**

## GOGI GROUP MEMBERS

The finest GOGI members encourage others to participate and are patient with the process of group study. The finest group members respect what is shared in their group as private and personal, and they treat others as they would like others to treat them. The finest group members offer positive support and encouragement.

## OBJECTIVE OF GOGI STUDY

The objective of all GOGI study is to empower the individual with evidence-based and proven cognitive tools for positive decision-making. The learning of each of these tools is measured by the understanding and the daily use of the GOGI TOOLS FOR POSITIVE DECISION-MAKING.

At the front of this workbook you will find the DO YOU KNOW YOUR GOGI recap. These are the answers to questions our students were asked when they went to Board. When you know the information on the DO YOU KNOW YOUR GOGI pages, you can clearly articulate what you have learned during your GOGI Study Group. It will be helpful to have students read the DO YOU KNOW YOUR GOGI pages during each GOGI Group meeting. This will reinforce the objectives of the group.

## WHO CREATED GOGI'S OFFICIAL MEETING FORMAT, AND WHY?

Prisoners with experience in many different types of group meetings created the official meeting format. It is used so all GOGI meetings follow a uniform format that is familiar to anyone attending meetings in different locations. This book has the official GOGI meeting for your group follow each week.

## A WORTHY GOAL

Your GOGI Group is a unique opportunity for you to unite with a small group of individuals who will be making better decisions in their lives.

Your GOGI Group will be considered among the finest if, at the end of this cycle, each member:

1)   TOOLS – Can recite the tools from memory.
2)   PLEDGE – Can recite the pledge from memory.
3)   CALENDAR – Knows why we, as a GOGI Nation, ALWAYS study on calendar.

*And remember...*

**GOGI-4-Life!**
***GOGI is not a course...GOGI is a culture!***

# The GOGI Pledge

*May our commitment (repeat)*

*To the study of GOGI (repeat)*

*Grant us the joy (repeat)*

*Of giving and receiving (repeat)*

*So that our inner freedom (repeat)*

*May be of maximum service (repeat)*

*To those we love (repeat)*

*And infinite others (repeat)*

## DAILY SIGN-IN – GROUP CERTIFICATE COURSE
**If you want to receive credit, please fill out the information below:**

The month is_____ The day of the month is _____ The year is_____ Signature _____
Meeting location_____ Start time _____ Number of people in my Group _____
**MY GROUP STUDIES ACCORDING TO THE GOGI CALENDAR (circle one)   YES   NO**

# A Quick Review of the GOGI Meeting Format

**Let's quickly review the elements of an official GOGI meeting. This week have volunteers simply read through each part so you are better prepared for next week.**

Please circle the week you are holding the (TOOL NAME) meeting.

(The weeks to study this week's GOGI Tool will be listed here.)

**Remember, because you will study GOGI according to The GOGI Calendar, you will turn to the correct page in this workbook. You MAY start at the END of this book. STUDY ON CALENDAR.**

## Call Your Meeting to Order

*To be read by a volunteer:*

We call this GOGI meeting to order. We are gathered here today as a GOGI community of like-minded individuals who CLAIM RESPONSIBILITY for our lives in our own unique ways. We include the GOGI TOOLS FOR POSITIVE DECISION-MAKING as a supplement to our existing or potential spiritual and social support systems. We believe that the GOGI Tools help us on our journey toward internal freedom regardless of any perceived differences among us. We realize the GOGI TOOLS FOR POSITIVE DECISION-MAKING are learned according to a calendar and they are simple tools that may enhance many other practices that promote our health and well-being. We acknowledge the GOGI Tools as positive decision-making tools to help us in our daily living.

## The GOGI Purpose

*To be read by a volunteer:*

The purpose of GOGI is to provide simple tools to anyone interested in making more positive decisions in their lives. We do this through sharing the GOGI Tools which are taught in many ways and formats including independent-study, small group study, as well as formal educational programming offering course credit provided by institutions or educational organizations. Our purpose is to offer these tools as a positive and prosocial culture, not as a program, even in instances where GOGI is studied in a program format. We study the GOGI Tools according to the GOGI Calendar so no one will ever be alone in their study of GOGI. The GOGI Tools are to be shared freely among all people and should not be withheld for any reason.

## Reading of Your Tools *(To be read by a volunteer:)*

## The GOGI TOOLS FOR POSITIVE DECISION-MAKING are:

| | |
|---|---|
| BOSS OF MY BRAIN | CLAIM RESPONSIBILITY |
| BELLY BREATHING | LET GO |
| FIVE SECOND LIGHTSWITCH | FOR–GIVE |
| POSITIVE THOUGHTS | WHAT IF |
| POSITIVE WORDS | REALITY CHECK |
| POSITIVE ACTIONS | ULTIMATE FREEDOM |

## DAILY SIGN-IN – GROUP CERTIFICATE COURSE
**If you want to receive credit, please fill out the information below:**

The month is_____ The day of the month is _____ The year is_____ Signature _____

Meeting location_____ Start time _____ Number of people in my Group _____

**MY GROUP STUDIES ACCORDING TO THE GOGI CALENDAR (circle one)    YES    NO**

## This Week's Objective

*To be read by a volunteer:*

(Individual tool OBJECTIVE will be listed here.)

## Check in/Recap of Your Prior Week

A brief check in when group members share their progress with the tools.

## Your Group Discussion

Please have volunteers or preassigned group members read from any of the GOGI books. This can be anything from any of the GOGI books related to the tool of this week (according to the GOGI Calendar). You may wish to have multiple people read from different GOGI books.

## Your Group Questions and Activities

This is a perfect time to have an activity. Your group can discuss this tool and, if completing GOGI as a program for credit, now is a great time to review or have your group members complete the required reading in this workbook.

## Close Your Meeting

*(volunteer to read) We invite you to join us for our next meeting to be held (date) where we will study the GOGI Tool: _____ (refer to Calendar). If we are unable to hold next week's meeting we will refer to the Calendar for the tool we will study at the next meeting. Course credit is earned by meeting twelve to fifteen times, even if tools are skipped or repeated.*

## GOGI Pledge

*To be read by a volunteer:*

*May our commitment (group repeat)*
*To the study of GOGI (group repeat)*
*Grant us the joy (group repeat)*
*Of giving and receiving (group repeat)*
*So that our inner freedom (group repeat)*
*May be of maximum service (group repeat)*
*To those we love (group repeat)*
*And infinite others (group repeat)*

## Next Week

*(volunteer to read) You have completed week one of GOGI. See you next week. Check your calendar to see which tool you will study next week. GO GOGI!*

# REMAIN ON THE GOGI CALENDAR

## Start the BOSS OF MY BRAIN Meeting in 3 easy Steps

1. Check the **GOGI Calendar** before your meeting

2. Read the **GOGI Tools Basics** before your meeting

3. Enjoy your **GOGI Meeting**

# The GOGI BOSS OF MY BRAIN Calendar
## For all GOGI meetings, remain on the GOGI calendar.

GOGI studies all tools according to the CALENDAR. GOGI weeks always start on Monday. Each month will start on Monday the 1st, 2nd, 3rd, 4th, 5th, 6th, or 7th. BOSS OF MY BRAIN is studied by all GOGI students on the weeks circled below. Fifteen meetings makes one cycle of study. You might study one tool twice if a meeting was missed. That's okay!

### JANUARY
Week 1 BOSS OF MY BRAIN
Week 2 BELLY BREATHING
Week 3 FIVE SECOND LIGHTSWITCH
Week 4 POSITIVE THOUGHTS
Week 5 REVIEW ABOVE

### FEBRUARY
Week 1 POSITIVE WORDS
Week 2 POSITIVE ACTIONS
Week 3 CLAIM RESPONSIBILITY
Week 4 LET GO
Week 5 REVIEW ABOVE

### MARCH
Week 1 FOR-GIVE
Week 2 WHAT IF
Week 3 REALITY CHECK
Week 4 ULTIMATE FREEDOM
Week 5 REVIEW ABOVE

### APRIL
Week 1 BOSS OF MY BRAIN
Week 2 BELLY BREATHING
Week 3 FIVE SECOND LIGHTSWITCH
Week 4 POSITIVE THOUGHTS
Week 5 REVIEW ABOVE

### MAY
Week 1 POSITIVE WORDS
Week 2 POSITIVE ACTIONS
Week 3 CLAIM RESPONSIBILITY
Week 4 LET GO
Week 5 REVIEW ABOVE

### JUNE
Week 1 FOR-GIVE
Week 2 WHAT IF
Week 3 REALITY CHECK
Week 4 ULTIMATE FREEDOM
Week 5 REVIEW ABOVE

### JULY
Week 1 BOSS OF MY BRAIN
Week 2 BELLY BREATHING
Week 3 FIVE SECOND LIGHTSWITCH
Week 4 POSITIVE THOUGHTS
Week 5 REVIEW ABOVE

### AUGUST
Week 1 POSITIVE WORDS
Week 2 POSITIVE ACTIONS
Week 3 CLAIM RESPONSIBILITY
Week 4 LET GO
Week 5 REVIEW ABOVE

### SEPTEMBER
Week 1 FOR-GIVE
Week 2 WHAT IF
Week 3 REALITY CHECK
Week 4 ULTIMATE FREEDOM
Week 5 REVIEW ABOVE

### OCTOBER
Week 1 BOSS OF MY BRAIN
Week 2 BELLY BREATHING
Week 3 FIVE SECOND LIGHTSWITCH
Week 4 POSITIVE THOUGHTS
Week 5 REVIEW ABOVE

### NOVEMBER
Week 1 POSITIVE WORDS
Week 2 POSITIVE ACTIONS
Week 3 CLAIM RESPONSIBILITY
Week 4 LET GO
Week 5 REVIEW ABOVE

### DECEMBER
Week 1 FOR-GIVE
Week 2 WHAT IF
Week 3 REALITY CHECK
Week 4 ULTIMATE FREEDOM
Week 5 REVIEW ABOVE

# BOSS OF MY BRAIN Basics

## Check the week you are holding this group study:

_____ 1st Week of January

_____ 1st Week of April

_____ 1st Week of July

_____ 1st Week of October

## KEYWORDS – BOSS OF MY BRAIN

THE THREE PARTS

There are three parts that matter: SMART PART, EMOTIONAL PART, and the OLD HABIT PART. Which one is the boss right now?

## STATEMENT OF PURPOSE AND OWNERSHIP – BOSS OF MY BRAIN

I am BOSS OF MY BRAIN and I have complete control over each thought I create. Because I am BOSS OF MY BRAIN, I can change my thoughts at any time. No one has control over my thoughts because only I am the BOSS OF MY BRAIN.

## OBJECTIVE – BOSS OF MY BRAIN

Your goal with this week's tool is to learn that you have a choice in how your brain thinks. You can SMART think, EMOTIONAL think, or you can OLD HABIT think. You are the boss of how you think and you will learn how to be the boss with this week's tool called BOSS OF MY BRAIN.

## TOOL INTRO – BOSS OF MY BRAIN

Did you know that GOGI believes there are only three parts of your brain you need to understand? At GOGI we focus on these three parts of your brain:

- **The SMART PART**
- **The EMOTIONAL PART**
- **The OLD HABIT PART**

**DAILY SIGN-IN – GROUP CERTIFICATE COURSE**
If you want to receive credit, please fill out the information below:
The month is_____1_____ The day of the month is ____4____ The year is _20_ Signature _____
Meeting location_____ Start time _____ Number of people in my Group _____
MY GROUP STUDIES ACCORDING TO THE GOGI CALENDAR (circle one)    YES    NO

## HOW TO USE – BOSS OF MY BRAIN

If you want to use the GOGI TOOL called BOSS OF MY BRAIN, all you need to do is ask yourself, "What part of my brain is in charge right now?" It's that simple.

- The **SMART PART** of your brain is where you learn new things. This is the part of the brain that will help you be strong and make positive decisions.

- The **EMOTIONAL PART** is filled with opinions, drama, anger, or hurt. When you let this part of your brain be the boss, you are not going to make positive decisions.

- The **OLD HABIT PART** of your brain is where all those old habits you no longer need are stored. The less you rely on old habits, the more room you will have for the SMART PART to help you create new positive habits.

## TELL US WHAT YOU JUST READ

You have just finished reading the BOSS OF MY BRAIN Basics. The Basics consist of the weeks you study BOSS OF MY BRAIN, the KEYWORDS, STATEMENT OF PURPOSE AND OWNERSHIP, OBJECTIVE, TOOL INTRO and HOW TO USE BOSS OF MY BRAIN. Remember ALL GOGI Tools were written **by** prisoners **for** prisoners.

*In your own words, explain the GOGI Tool BOSS OF MY BRAIN:* _____

_____

_____

_____

_____

_____

_____

_____

**DAILY SIGN-IN – GROUP CERTIFICATE COURSE**
If you want to receive credit, please fill out the information below:

The month is _H_ The day of the month is _4_ The year is _20_ Signature _____
Meeting location _____ Start time _____ Number of people in my Group _____
MY GROUP STUDIES ACCORDING TO THE GOGI CALENDAR (circle one)   YES   NO

# BOSS OF MY BRAIN Meeting

GOGI weeks begin on Monday. ONLY hold this meeting in the following weeks: (check the week you are studying the BOSS OF MY BRAIN Tool.)

❏1st week of January  ❏1st week of April  ❏1st week of July  ❏1st week of October

## Call Your Meeting to Order

*To be read by a volunteer:*
We call this GOGI meeting to order. We are gathered here today as a GOGI community of like-minded individuals who CLAIM RESPONSIBILITY for our lives in our own unique ways. We include the GOGI TOOLS FOR POSITIVE DECISION-MAKING as a supplement to our existing or potential spiritual and social support systems. We believe that the GOGI Tools help us on our journey toward internal freedom regardless of any perceived differences among us. We realize the GOGI TOOLS FOR POSITIVE DECISION-MAKING are learned according to a calendar and they are simple tools that may enhance many other practices that promote our health and well-being. We acknowledge the GOGI Tools as positive decision-making tools to help us in our daily living.

## The GOGI Purpose

*To be read by a volunteer:*
The purpose of GOGI is to provide simple tools to anyone interested in making more positive decisions in their lives. We do this through sharing the GOGI Tools which are taught in many ways and formats including independent-study, small group study, as well as formal educational programming offering course credit provided by institutions or educational organizations. Our purpose is to offer these tools as a positive and prosocial culture, not as a program, even in instances where GOGI is studied in a program format. We study the GOGI Tools according to the GOGI Calendar so no one will ever be alone in their study of GOGI. The GOGI Tools are to be shared freely among all people and should not be withheld for any reason.

## Reading of Your Tools *(To be read by a volunteer:)*
## The **GOGI TOOLS FOR POSITIVE DECISION-MAKING** are:

| | |
|---|---|
| BOSS OF MY BRAIN | CLAIM RESPONSIBILITY |
| BELLY BREATHING | LET GO |
| FIVE SECOND LIGHTSWITCH | FOR–GIVE |
| POSITIVE THOUGHTS | WHAT IF |
| POSITIVE WORDS | REALITY CHECK |
| POSITIVE ACTIONS | ULTIMATE FREEDOM |

**DAILY SIGN-IN – GROUP CERTIFICATE COURSE**
If you want to receive credit, please fill out the information below:

The month is ___1___ The day of the month is ___4___ The year is __2O__ Signature _____
Meeting location_____ Start time _____ Number of people in my Group _____
MY GROUP STUDIES ACCORDING TO THE GOGI CALENDAR (circle one)    YES    NO

## This Week's Objective

*To be read by a volunteer:*
According to the GOGI calendar, the tool of this week is BOSS OF MY BRAIN. Your goal is to learn that you have a choice in how your brain thinks. You can SMART think, EMOTIONAL think, or OLD HABIT think. You are the boss of how you think. You will learn how to be the boss with this week's tool called BOSS OF MY BRAIN.

## Check in/Recap of Your Prior Week

A brief check in when group members share their progress with the tools.

## Your Group Discussion

Please have volunteers or preassigned group members read from any of the GOGI books. This can be anything from any of the GOGI books related to the tool of this week (according to the GOGI Calendar). You may wish to have multiple people read from different GOGI books.

## Your Group Questions and Activities

This is a perfect time to have an activity. Your group can discuss this tool and, if completing GOGI as a program for credit, now is a great time to review or have your group members complete any required written assignments.

## Close Your Meeting

*We invite you to join us for our next meeting to be held (date) where we will study the GOGI Tool: _____ (refer to Calendar). If we are unable to hold next week's meeting we will refer to the Calendar for the tool we will study at the next meeting. Course credit is earned by meeting twelve to fifteen times, even if tools are skipped or repeated.*

## GOGI Pledge

*To be read by a volunteer:*

> *May our commitment (group repeat)*
> *To the study of GOGI (group repeat)*
> *Grant us the joy (group repeat)*
> *Of giving and receiving (group repeat)*
> *So that our inner freedom (group repeat)*
> *May be of maximum service (group repeat)*
> *To those we love (group repeat)*
> *And infinite others (group repeat)*

This art is a gift to GOGI from Dana Harper, a free man in 2018.

## Weekly Course Worksheet BOSS OF MY BRAIN

*Now that you have read the BOSS OF MY BRAIN KEYWORDS, which part of your brain do you think you used most frequently in the past? Why?* _____

_____

_____

*What do you like most about the BOSS OF MY BRAIN tool?* _____

_____

_____

_____

*How can the BOSS OF MY BRAIN tool help you make more positive decisions?* _____

_____

_____

*What will help you to remember the BOSS OF MY BRAIN tool?* _____

_____

*We learn new things all the time, why is it so hard for some people to remember the BOSS OF MY BRAIN Tool when they are angry?* _____

_____

_____

*What might improve in your life if you used the SMART PART of your brain more and the OLD HABIT PART less?* _____

_____

_____

*Do you think the old saying 'practice makes perfect' applies to this and all GOGI Tools? Why?* _____

_____

_____

## DAILY SIGN-IN – GROUP CERTIFICATE COURSE
### If you want to receive credit, please fill out the information below:

The month is ___1___ The day of the month is ___4___ The year is _20_ Signature _____

Meeting location_____ Start time _____ Number of people in my Group _____

MY GROUP STUDIES ACCORDING TO THE GOGI CALENDAR (circle one)     YES     NO

## My GOGI Group Reflections

In my GOGI Group this week I learned about the tool: _____

_____

This tool belongs to the section of tools called: The Tools of _____

I learned that this GOGI Tool has KEYWORDS. The KEYWORDS for this tool are:

_____

_____

If I choose, I could apply this GOGI Tool to my daily life. Below is an example of how this tool might help me make better decisions:_____

_____

_____

_____

What I liked most about my GOGI Group this week was: _____

_____

_____

Meeting in a GOGI Group is helpful to my learning and growth because: _____

_____

_____

Here are some things I want to write down so that I do not forget them in the future. They are my thoughts and my observations about life and GOGI. _____

_____

_____

_____

_____

_____

# REMAIN ON THE GOGI CALENDAR

## Start the BELLY BREATHING
## Meeting in 3 easy Steps

1. Check the **GOGI Calendar** before your meeting

2. Read the **GOGI Tools Basics** before your meeting

3. Enjoy your **GOGI Meeting**

# The GOGI BELLY BREATHING Calendar
## For all GOGI meetings, remain on the GOGI calendar.

GOGI studies all tools according to the CALENDAR. GOGI weeks always start on Monday. Each month will start on Monday the 1st, 2nd, 3rd, 4th, 5th, 6th, or 7th. BELLY BREATHING is studied by all GOGI students on the weeks circled below. Fifteen meetings makes one cycle of study. You might study one tool twice if a meeting was missed. That's okay!

### JANUARY
Week 1 BOSS OF MY BRAIN
Week 2 BELLY BREATHING
Week 3 FIVE SECOND LIGHTSWITCH
Week 4 POSITIVE THOUGHTS
Week 5 REVIEW ABOVE

### FEBRUARY
Week 1 POSITIVE WORDS
Week 2 POSITIVE ACTIONS
Week 3 CLAIM RESPONSIBILITY
Week 4 LET GO
Week 5 REVIEW ABOVE

### MARCH
Week 1 FOR–GIVE
Week 2 WHAT IF
Week 3 REALITY CHECK
Week 4 ULTIMATE FREEDOM
Week 5 REVIEW ABOVE

### APRIL
Week 1 BOSS OF MY BRAIN
Week 2 BELLY BREATHING
Week 3 FIVE SECOND LIGHTSWITCH
Week 4 POSITIVE THOUGHTS
Week 5 REVIEW ABOVE

### MAY
Week 1 POSITIVE WORDS
Week 2 POSITIVE ACTIONS
Week 3 CLAIM RESPONSIBILITY
Week 4 LET GO
Week 5 REVIEW ABOVE

### JUNE
Week 1 FOR–GIVE
Week 2 WHAT IF
Week 3 REALITY CHECK
Week 4 ULTIMATE FREEDOM
Week 5 REVIEW ABOVE

### JULY
Week 1 BOSS OF MY BRAIN
Week 2 BELLY BREATHING
Week 3 FIVE SECOND LIGHTSWITCH
Week 4 POSITIVE THOUGHTS
Week 5 REVIEW ABOVE

### AUGUST
Week 1 POSITIVE WORDS
Week 2 POSITIVE ACTIONS
Week 3 CLAIM RESPONSIBILITY
Week 4 LET GO
Week 5 REVIEW ABOVE

### SEPTEMBER
Week 1 FOR–GIVE
Week 2 WHAT IF
Week 3 REALITY CHECK
Week 4 ULTIMATE FREEDOM
Week 5 REVIEW ABOVE

### OCTOBER
Week 1 BOSS OF MY BRAIN
Week 2 BELLY BREATHING
Week 3 FIVE SECOND LIGHTSWITCH
Week 4 POSITIVE THOUGHTS
Week 5 REVIEW ABOVE

### NOVEMBER
Week 1 POSITIVE WORDS
Week 2 POSITIVE ACTIONS
Week 3 CLAIM RESPONSIBILITY
Week 4 LET GO
Week 5 REVIEW ABOVE

### DECEMBER
Week 1 FOR–GIVE
Week 2 WHAT IF
Week 3 REALITY CHECK
Week 4 ULTIMATE FREEDOM
Week 5 REVIEW ABOVE

**DAILY SIGN-IN – GROUP CERTIFICATE COURSE**
If you want to receive credit, please fill out the information below:

The month is ___1___  The day of the month is ___11___  The year is _20_ Signature _____

Meeting location_____ Start time _____ Number of people in my Group _____

MY GROUP STUDIES ACCORDING TO THE GOGI CALENDAR (circle one)    YES    NO

# BELLY BREATHING Basics

## Check the week you are holding this group study:

____ 2nd Week of January

____ 2nd Week of April

____ 2nd Week of July

____ 2nd Week of October

## KEYWORDS – BELLY BREATHING

ONE HAND ON MY CHEST, ONE HAND ON MY BELLY. WHICH ONE IS MOVING RIGHT NOW? My brain works better when my belly moves.

## STATEMENT OF PURPOSE AND OWNERSHIP – BELLY BREATHING

With BELLY BREATHING I can instantly relax my body and I can make positive decisions. When I am BELLY BREATHING, I take control of my thoughts and feelings.

## OBJECTIVE – BELLY BREATHING

Your goal in learning this week's tool is to breathe with your chest remaining still and your belly moving in and out. This is your most powerful way to breathe and you can achieve this with this week's tool called BELLY BREATHING.

## TOOL INTRO – BELLY BREATHING

Did you know that when you breathe with your belly, it actually makes you smarter? It is true. This is because when you breathe into your belly you are also getting oxygen into your brain, and that makes the brain work better. GOGI believes there are two types of breathing: breathing with your chest, and BELLY BREATHING.

## HOW TO USE – BELLY BREATHING

You can use the BELLY BREATHING tool at any time. Here are three ways to use the tool:

- You can actually put one hand on your chest and one hand on your stomach and see which one is moving.

- Or, just put one hand on your stomach to make sure it is moving.

- If you are breathing with your chest, you can direct the air all the way into your stomach area and begin BELLY BREATHING.

## TELL US WHAT YOU JUST READ

You have just finished reading the BELLY BREATHING Basics. The Basics consist of the weeks you study BELLY BREATHING, the KEYWORDS, STATEMENT OF PURPOSE AND OWNERSHIP, OBJECTIVE, TOOL INTRO and HOW TO USE BELLY BREATHING. Remember ALL GOGI Tools were written **by** prisoners *fo*r prisoners.

In your own words, explain the GOGI Tool BELLY BREATHING:

_____

_____

_____

_____

_____

_____

_____

# BELLY BREATHING Meeting

GOGI weeks begin on Monday. ONLY hold this meeting in the following weeks: (check the week you are studying the BELLY BREATHING Tool.)

❑ 2nd week of January  ❑ 2nd week of April  ❑ 2nd week of July  ❑ 2nd week of October

## Call Your Meeting to Order

*To be read by a volunteer:*

We call this GOGI meeting to order. We are gathered here today as a GOGI community of like-minded individuals who CLAIM RESPONSIBILITY for our lives in our own unique ways. We include the GOGI TOOLS FOR POSITIVE DECISION-MAKING as a supplement to our existing or potential spiritual and social support systems. We believe that the GOGI Tools help us on our journey toward internal freedom regardless of any perceived differences among us. We realize the GOGI TOOLS FOR POSITIVE DECISION-MAKING are learned according to a calendar and they are simple tools that may enhance many other practices that promote our health and well-being. We acknowledge the GOGI Tools as positive decision-making tools to help us in our daily living.

## The GOGI Purpose

*To be read by a volunteer:*

The purpose of GOGI is to provide simple tools to anyone interested in making more positive decisions in their lives. We do this through sharing the GOGI Tools which are taught in many ways and formats including independent-study, small group study, as well as formal educational programming offering course credit provided by institutions or educational organizations. Our purpose is to offer these tools as a positive and prosocial culture, not as a program, even in instances where GOGI is studied in a program format. We study the GOGI Tools according to the GOGI Calendar so no one will ever be alone in their study of GOGI. The GOGI Tools are to be shared freely among all people and should not be withheld for any reason.

## Reading of Your Tools *(To be read by a volunteer:)*

## The GOGI TOOLS FOR POSITIVE DECISION-MAKING are:

| | |
|---|---|
| BOSS OF MY BRAIN | CLAIM RESPONSIBILITY |
| BELLY BREATHING | LET GO |
| FIVE SECOND LIGHTSWITCH | FOR–GIVE |
| POSITIVE THOUGHTS | WHAT IF |
| POSITIVE WORDS | REALITY CHECK |
| POSITIVE ACTIONS | ULTIMATE FREEDOM |

## DAILY SIGN-IN – GROUP CERTIFICATE COURSE
### If you want to receive credit, please fill out the information below:

The month is __\__ The day of the month is __\ \__ The year is _ᒿ०_ Signature _____

Meeting location_____ Start time _____ Number of people in my Group _____

**MY GROUP STUDIES ACCORDING TO THE GOGI CALENDAR (circle one)   YES   NO**

## This Week's Objective

*To be read by a volunteer:*
Your goal in learning this week's tool is for you to breathe with your chest remaining still and your belly moving in and out. This is your most powerful way to breathe and you can achieve this with this week's tool called BELLY BREATHING. BELLY BREATHING will help you make more positive decisions because when you get air into your belly, your brain works better.

## Check in/Recap of Your Prior Week

A brief check in when group members share their progress with the tools.

## Your Group Discussion

Please have volunteers or preassigned group members read from any of the GOGI books. This can be anything from any of the GOGI books related to the tool of this week (according to the GOGI Calendar). You may wish to have multiple people read from different GOGI books.

## Your Group Questions and Activities

This is a perfect time to have an activity. Your group can discuss this tool and, if completing GOGI as a program for credit, now is a great time to review or have your group members complete any required written assignments.

## Close Your Meeting

*We invite you to join us for our next meeting to be held (date) where we will study the GOGI Tool: _____ (refer to Calendar). If we are unable to hold next week's meeting we will refer to the Calendar for the tool we will study at the next meeting. Course credit is earned by meeting twelve to fifteen times, even if tools are skipped or repeated.*

## GOGI Pledge

*To be read by a volunteer:*
> *May our commitment (group repeat)*
> *To the study of GOGI (group repeat)*
> *Grant us the joy (group repeat)*
> *Of giving and receiving (group repeat)*
> *So that our inner freedom (group repeat)*
> *May be of maximum service (group repeat)*
> *To those we love (group repeat)*
> *And infinite others (group repeat)*

Art is a gift from Daniel O.

## Weekly Course Worksheet BELLY BREATHING

*When you read MY BRAIN WORKS BETTER WHEN MY BELLY MOVES in the KEYWORDS, do think this is true? And why?* _____

_____

_____

*What is the most difficult part of BELLY BREATHING?* _____

_____

_____

*Most people don't realize that there are two ways to breathe: with your chest and BELLY BREATHING. When you are BELLY BREATHING, what happens physically in your body?* _____

_____

_____

*Why do you think so many people say that BELLY BREATHING help them make more positive decisions?*_____

_____

_____

_____

*How would you explain BELLY BREATHING to a teenager? Why would it be important for a teenager to use BELLY BREATHING?* _____

_____

_____

_____

_____

_____

## My Gift to GOGI ~ my art, poem or activity

My signature _____ ID number _____ Location _____
Print your name Robert Baldasaro

## My Gift to GOGI ~ my art, poem or activity

My signature _____ Woody W. Hartman _____ ID number _____ Location _____
Print your name Woody Hartman

The month is _____ The day of the month is ___\\___ The year is ___∠◯___ Signature _____

Meeting location_____ Start time _____ Number of people in my Group _____

**MY GROUP STUDIES ACCORDING TO THE GOGI CALENDAR (circle one)    YES    NO**

## My GOGI Group Reflections

*In my GOGI Group this week I learned about the tool:* _____

_____

*This tool belongs to the section of tools called: The Tools of* _____

*I learned that this GOGI Tool has KEYWORDS. The KEYWORDS for this tool are:*

_____

_____

_____

*If I choose, I could apply this GOGI Tool to my daily life. Below is an example of how this tool might help me make better decisions:*_____

_____

_____

_____

*What I liked most about my GOGI Group this week was:* _____

_____

_____

*Meeting in a GOGI Group is helpful to my learning and growth because:* _____

_____

_____

*Here are some things I want to write down so that I do not forget them in the future. They are my thoughts and my observations about life and GOGI.* _____

_____

_____

_____

_____

# REMAIN ON THE GOGI CALENDAR

## Start the
## FIVE SECOND LIGHTSWITCH
## Meeting in 3 easy Steps

1. **Check the GOGI Calendar before your meeting**

2. **Read the GOGI Tools Basics before your meeting**

3. **Enjoy your GOGI Meeting**

# The GOGI FIVE SECOND LIGHTSWITCH Calendar
## For all GOGI meetings, remain on the GOGI calendar.

GOGI studies all tools according to the CALENDAR. GOGI weeks always start on Monday. Each month will start on Monday the 1st, 2nd, 3rd, 4th, 5th, 6th, or 7th. FIVE SECOND LIGHTSWITCH is studied by all GOGI students on the weeks circled below. Fifteen meetings makes one cycle of study. You might study one tool twice if a meeting was missed. That's okay!

### JANUARY
Week 1 BOSS OF MY BRAIN
Week 2 BELLY BREATHING
Week 3 FIVE SECOND LIGHTSWITCH
Week 4 POSITIVE THOUGHTS
Week 5 REVIEW ABOVE

### FEBRUARY
Week 1 POSITIVE WORDS
Week 2 POSITIVE ACTIONS
Week 3 CLAIM RESPONSIBILITY
Week 4 LET GO
Week 5 REVIEW ABOVE

### MARCH
Week 1 FOR-GIVE
Week 2 WHAT IF
Week 3 REALITY CHECK
Week 4 ULTIMATE FREEDOM
Week 5 REVIEW ABOVE

### APRIL
Week 1 BOSS OF MY BRAIN
Week 2 BELLY BREATHING
Week 3 FIVE SECOND LIGHTSWITCH
Week 4 POSITIVE THOUGHTS
Week 5 REVIEW ABOVE

### MAY
Week 1 POSITIVE WORDS
Week 2 POSITIVE ACTIONS
Week 3 CLAIM RESPONSIBILITY
Week 4 LET GO
Week 5 REVIEW ABOVE

### JUNE
Week 1 FOR-GIVE
Week 2 WHAT IF
Week 3 REALITY CHECK
Week 4 ULTIMATE FREEDOM
Week 5 REVIEW ABOVE

### JULY
Week 1 BOSS OF MY BRAIN
Week 2 BELLY BREATHING
Week 3 FIVE SECOND LIGHTSWITCH
Week 4 POSITIVE THOUGHTS
Week 5 REVIEW ABOVE

### AUGUST
Week 1 POSITIVE WORDS
Week 2 POSITIVE ACTIONS
Week 3 CLAIM RESPONSIBILITY
Week 4 LET GO
Week 5 REVIEW ABOVE

### SEPTEMBER
Week 1 FOR-GIVE
Week 2 WHAT IF
Week 3 REALITY CHECK
Week 4 ULTIMATE FREEDOM
Week 5 REVIEW ABOVE

### OCTOBER
Week 1 BOSS OF MY BRAIN
Week 2 BELLY BREATHING
Week 3 FIVE SECOND LIGHTSWITCH
Week 4 POSITIVE THOUGHTS
Week 5 REVIEW ABOVE

### NOVEMBER
Week 1 POSITIVE WORDS
Week 2 POSITIVE ACTIONS
Week 3 CLAIM RESPONSIBILITY
Week 4 LET GO
Week 5 REVIEW ABOVE

### DECEMBER
Week 1 FOR-GIVE
Week 2 WHAT IF
Week 3 REALITY CHECK
Week 4 ULTIMATE FREEDOM
Week 5 REVIEW ABOVE

**DAILY SIGN-IN – GROUP CERTIFICATE COURSE**
If you want to receive credit, please fill out the information below:
The month is ___1___ The day of the month is ___18___ The year is __20__ Signature _____
Meeting location_____ Start time _____ Number of people in my Group _____
MY GROUP STUDIES ACCORDING TO THE GOGI CALENDAR (circle one)     YES     NO

# FIVE SECOND LIGHTSWITCH Basics

## Check the week you are holding this group study:

_____ 3rd Week of January

_____ 3rd Week of April

_____ 3rd Week of July

_____ 3rd Week of October

## KEYWORDS – FIVE SECOND LIGHTSWITCH

OLD THOUGHT = NEW ACTION.

I have an OLD THOUGHT and I have a NEW ACTION.

## STATEMENT OF PURPOSE AND OWNERSHIP – FIVE SECOND LIGHTSWITCH

I can flip my FIVE SECOND LIGHTSWITCH and instantly change any negative thought to a positive action. There is no negative thought more powerful than my positive action when I flip my FIVE SECOND LIGHTSWITCH.

## OBJECTIVE – FIVE SECOND LIGHTSWITCH

Your goal this week is to build the habit of choosing a new positive action every time you have an old negative thought. You can do this by using your FIVE SECOND LIGHTSWITCH, which is this week's tool.

## TOOL INTRO – FIVE SECOND LIGHTSWITCH

Here is an example. When you are told, "just don't think about smoking a cigarette," it seems that all you can think about is the cigarette. When beginning to train your mind to create other thoughts, it is nearly impossible to think that you could simply stop thinking about something that consumed a lot of thinking for a long time.

FIVE SECOND LIGHTSWITCH works. This tool helps you realize that your mind has been trained to head down a particular road, almost like autopilot. The GOGI

Tool FIVE SECOND LIGHTSWITCH permits you to observe that thought, and then replace that thought with a new, more positive and productive action.

At GOGI we call this flipping the FIVE SECOND LIGHTSWITCH. This tool provides you with the power to reroute your brain activity so you can be stronger in your positive choices.

## HOW TO USE – FIVE SECOND LIGHTSWITCH

You can use the FIVE SECOND LIGHTSWITCH tool when your thoughts seem to be the boss of you. When an urge seems really really strong, the FIVE SECOND LIGHTSWITCH is a powerful tool to use.

The key to FIVE SECOND LIGHTSWITCH is to have your replacement action ready. If you have your replacement action ready, you are likely to have great success with FIVE SECOND LIGHTSWITCH.

## TELL US WHAT YOU JUST READ

You have just finished reading the FIVE SECOND LIGHTSWITCH Basics. The Basics consist of the weeks you study FIVE SECOND LIGHTSWITCH, the KEYWORDS, STATEMENT OF PURPOSE AND OWNERSHIP, OBJECTIVE, TOOL INTRO and HOW TO USE FIVE SECOND LIGHTSWITCH. Remember ALL GOGI Tools were written **by** prisoners **for** prisoners.

*In your own words, explain the GOGI Tool FIVE SECOND LIGHTSWITCH:* _____

_____

_____

_____

_____

_____

_____

# FIVE SECOND LIGHTSWITCH Meeting

GOGI weeks begin on Monday. ONLY hold this meeting in the following weeks: (check the week you are studying the FIVE SECOND LIGHTSWITCH Tool.)

❏ 3rd week of January   ❏ 3rd week of April   ❏ 3rd week of July   ❏ 3rd week of October

## Call Your Meeting to Order

*To be read by a volunteer:*

We call this GOGI meeting to order. We are gathered here today as a GOGI community of like-minded individuals who CLAIM RESPONSIBILITY for our lives in our own unique ways. We include the GOGI TOOLS FOR POSITIVE DECISION-MAKING as a supplement to our existing or potential spiritual and social support systems. We believe that the GOGI Tools help us on our journey toward internal freedom regardless of any perceived differences among us. We realize the GOGI TOOLS FOR POSITIVE DECISION-MAKING are learned according to a calendar and they are simple tools that may enhance many other practices that promote our health and well-being. We acknowledge the GOGI Tools as positive decision-making tools to help us in our daily living.

## The GOGI Purpose

*To be read by a volunteer:*

The purpose of GOGI is to provide simple tools to anyone interested in making more positive decisions in their lives. We do this through sharing the GOGI Tools which are taught in many ways and formats including independent-study, small group study, as well as formal educational programming offering course credit provided by institutions or educational organizations. Our purpose is to offer these tools as a positive and prosocial culture, not as a program, even in instances where GOGI is studied in a program format. We study the GOGI Tools according to the GOGI Calendar so no one will ever be alone in their study of GOGI. The GOGI Tools are to be shared freely among all people and should not be withheld for any reason.

## Reading of Your Tools *(To be read by a volunteer:)*

## The GOGI TOOLS FOR POSITIVE DECISION-MAKING are:

| | |
|---|---|
| BOSS OF MY BRAIN | CLAIM RESPONSIBILITY |
| BELLY BREATHING | LET GO |
| FIVE SECOND LIGHTSWITCH | FOR–GIVE |
| POSITIVE THOUGHTS | WHAT IF |
| POSITIVE WORDS | REALITY CHECK |
| POSITIVE ACTIONS | ULTIMATE FREEDOM |

## DAILY SIGN-IN – GROUP CERTIFICATE COURSE
**If you want to receive credit, please fill out the information below:**

The month is _____ The day of the month is 18 The year is 20 Signature _____
Meeting location_____ Start time _____ Number of people in my Group _____
MY GROUP STUDIES ACCORDING TO THE GOGI CALENDAR (circle one)    YES    NO

## This Week's Objective

*To be read by a volunteer:*
Your goal this week is to build the new habit of choosing a new positive action every time you have an old negative thought. You can do this by using your FIVE SECOND LIGHTSWITCH.

## Check in/Recap of Your Prior Week

A brief check in when group members share their progress with the tools.

## Your Group Discussion

Please have volunteers or preassigned group members read from any of the GOGI books. This can be anything from any of the GOGI books related to the tool of this week (according to the GOGI Calendar). You may wish to have multiple people read from different GOGI books.

## Your Group Questions and Activities

This is a perfect time to have an activity. Your group can discuss this tool and, if completing GOGI as a program for credit, now is a great time to review or have your group members complete any required written assignments.

## Close Your Meeting

*We invite you to join us for our next meeting to be held (date) where we will study the GOGI Tool: _____ (refer to Calendar). If we are unable to hold next week's meeting we will refer to the Calendar for the tool we will study at the next meeting. Course credit is earned by meeting twelve to fifteen times, even if tools are skipped or repeated.*

## GOGI Pledge

*To be read by a volunteer:*

*May our commitment (group repeat)*
*To the study of GOGI (group repeat)*
*Grant us the joy (group repeat)*
*Of giving and receiving (group repeat)*
*So that our inner freedom (group repeat)*
*May be of maximum service (group repeat)*
*To those we love (group repeat)*
*And infinite others (group repeat)*

# the real ricky m.

i asked myself the question what is
ULTIMATE FREEDOM. something that i'm
striving toward, something that i have
never experienced, because of the choice i
made to be a law breaker, instead of a law
abider. i know that my past lifestyle
wasn't freedom at all, knowing that i could
be in prison at any moment, playing the
game of russian roulette with my life.
always trying to stay one step ahead of
the law. where's the freedom in that? it
felt like freedom because my lifestyle
afforded me the selfish desires. this selfish
attitude was my ultimate undoing. thinking
about me and mines, was totally opposite
of what ULTIMATE FREEDOM required.
ULTIMATE FREEDOM teaches that my life
should be lived in service of others.
ULTIMATE FREEDOM is selfless, treating
others with love and kindness, living my life
how i want to be treated, as a fellow
human being, expressing my true character
through POSITIVE ACTIONS, POSITIVE
WORDS, POSITIVE THOUGHTS.

## DAILY SIGN-IN – GROUP CERTIFICATE COURSE
### If you want to receive credit, please fill out the information below:

The month is ___1___  The day of the month is __18__  The year is _20_  Signature _____

Meeting location_____ Start time _____ Number of people in my Group _____

MY GROUP STUDIES ACCORDING TO THE GOGI CALENDAR (circle one)   YES   NO

## Weekly Course Worksheet FIVE SECOND LIGHTSWITCH

*When you use the FIVE SECOND LIGHTSWITCH, what are 3 specific NEW ACTIONS you rely upon?*

1. _____

2. _____

3. _____

*Why is it important to have a NEW ACTION ready?* _____

_____

_____

*How can FIVE SECOND LIGHTSWITCH help those with old habits they wish to change?* _____

_____

_____

*Do you think that to "flip your FIVE SECOND LIGHTSWITCH" is a way to change your reactions? How and why?* _____

_____

_____

_____

_____

*What is a recent situation where using FIVE SECOND LIGHTSWITCH could be helpful to your progress. How might you flip the switch?* _____

_____

_____

_____

_____

_____

# My Gift to GOGI ~ my art, poem or activity

My signature _____ W. Hartman _____ ID number _____ Location _____
Print your name _____ Woody Hartman _____

Getting Out by Going In • P.O. Box 88969 • Los Angeles, CA 90009 • www.gettingoutbygoingin.org • 59

Use this page to answer the questions to the left. Answer any questions you wish, or all of the questions. Just fill the page with your thoughts.

## DAILY SIGN-IN – GROUP CERTIFICATE COURSE
**If you want to receive credit, please fill out the information below:**

The month is ___1___ The day of the month is __18__ The year is __20__ Signature _____

Meeting location_____ Start time _____ Number of people in my Group _____

**MY GROUP STUDIES ACCORDING TO THE GOGI CALENDAR (circle one)    YES    NO**

## My GOGI Group Reflections

*In my GOGI Group this week I learned about the tool:* _____

_____

*This tool belongs to the section of tools called: The Tools of* _____

*I learned that this GOGI Tool has KEYWORDS. The KEYWORDS for this tool are:*

_____

_____

_____

_____

*If I choose, I could apply this GOGI Tool to my daily life. Below is an example of how this tool might help me make better decisions:*_____

_____

_____

_____

*What I liked most about my GOGI Group this week was:* _____

_____

_____

*Meeting in a GOGI Group is helpful to my learning and growth because:* _____

_____

_____

*Here are some things I want to write down so that I do not forget them in the future. They are my thoughts and my observations about life and GOGI.* _____

_____

_____

_____

# REMAIN ON THE GOGI CALENDAR

## Start the POSITIVE THOUGHTS Meeting in 3 easy Steps

1. **Check the GOGI Calendar before your meeting**

2. **Read the GOGI Tools Basics before your meeting**

3. **Enjoy your GOGI Meeting**

# The GOGI POSITIVE THOUGHTS Calendar
## For all GOGI meetings, remain on the GOGI calendar.

GOGI studies all tools according to the CALENDAR. GOGI weeks always start on Monday. Each month will start on Monday the 1st, 2nd, 3rd, 4th, 5th, 6th, or 7th. POSITIVE THOUGHTS is studied by all GOGI students on the weeks circled below. Fifteen meetings makes one cycle of study. You might study one tool twice if a meeting was missed. That's okay!

### JANUARY
Week 1 BOSS OF MY BRAIN
Week 2 BELLY BREATHING
Week 3 FIVE SECOND LIGHTSWITCH
Week 4 POSITIVE THOUGHTS
Week 5 REVIEW ABOVE

### FEBRUARY
Week 1 POSITIVE WORDS
Week 2 POSITIVE ACTIONS
Week 3 CLAIM RESPONSIBILITY
Week 4 LET GO
Week 5 REVIEW ABOVE

### MARCH
Week 1 FOR-GIVE
Week 2 WHAT IF
Week 3 REALITY CHECK
Week 4 ULTIMATE FREEDOM
Week 5 REVIEW ABOVE

### APRIL
Week 1 BOSS OF MY BRAIN
Week 2 BELLY BREATHING
Week 3 FIVE SECOND LIGHTSWITCH
Week 4 POSITIVE THOUGHTS
Week 5 REVIEW ABOVE

### MAY
Week 1 POSITIVE WORDS
Week 2 POSITIVE ACTIONS
Week 3 CLAIM RESPONSIBILITY
Week 4 LET GO
Week 5 REVIEW ABOVE

### JUNE
Week 1 FOR-GIVE
Week 2 WHAT IF
Week 3 REALITY CHECK
Week 4 ULTIMATE FREEDOM
Week 5 REVIEW ABOVE

### JULY
Week 1 BOSS OF MY BRAIN
Week 2 BELLY BREATHING
Week 3 FIVE SECOND LIGHTSWITCH
Week 4 POSITIVE THOUGHTS
Week 5 REVIEW ABOVE

### AUGUST
Week 1 POSITIVE WORDS
Week 2 POSITIVE ACTIONS
Week 3 CLAIM RESPONSIBILITY
Week 4 LET GO
Week 5 REVIEW ABOVE

### SEPTEMBER
Week 1 FOR-GIVE
Week 2 WHAT IF
Week 3 REALITY CHECK
Week 4 ULTIMATE FREEDOM
Week 5 REVIEW ABOVE

### OCTOBER
Week 1 BOSS OF MY BRAIN
Week 2 BELLY BREATHING
Week 3 FIVE SECOND LIGHTSWITCH
Week 4 POSITIVE THOUGHTS
Week 5 REVIEW ABOVE

### NOVEMBER
Week 1 POSITIVE WORDS
Week 2 POSITIVE ACTIONS
Week 3 CLAIM RESPONSIBILITY
Week 4 LET GO
Week 5 REVIEW ABOVE

### DECEMBER
Week 1 FOR-GIVE
Week 2 WHAT IF
Week 3 REALITY CHECK
Week 4 ULTIMATE FREEDOM
Week 5 REVIEW ABOVE

# POSITIVE THOUGHTS Basics

## Check the week you are holding this group study:

_____ 4th Week of January

_____ 4th Week of April

_____ 4th Week of July

_____ 4th Week of October

## KEYWORDS – POSITIVE THOUGHTS

THE THREE Ps

Is it POWERFUL?

Is it PRODUCTIVE?

Is it POSITIVE?

## STATEMENT OF PURPOSE AND OWNERSHIP – POSITIVE THOUGHTS

My POSITIVE THOUGHTS set the direction of my life from this moment forward. I focus on POSITIVE THOUGHTS, even when it is difficult or challenging. No matter what is happening, I can create POSITIVE THOUGHTS.

## OBJECTIVE – POSITIVE THOUGHTS

Your goal with this week's tool is to practice being the boss of your thinking and to choose thoughts that are POWERFUL, PRODUCTIVE, and POSITIVE. You can practice this with the tool POSITIVE THOUGHTS.

## TOOL INTRO – POSITIVE THOUGHTS

You are the boss of your brain and you can create any thought you want to create. When you force your brain to create POSITIVE THOUGHTS, you are actually using the tool POSITIVE THOUGHTS.

Your brain will follow your orders and if you use the tool POSITIVE THOUGHTS over and over again, eventually your brain will begin to create POSITIVE THOUGHTS on its own.

**DAILY SIGN-IN – GROUP CERTIFICATE COURSE**
**If you want to receive credit, please fill out the information below:**
The month is ___1___   The day of the month is __25__   The year is __20__   Signature _____
Meeting location_____ Start time _____ Number of people in my Group _____
**MY GROUP STUDIES ACCORDING TO THE GOGI CALENDAR (circle one)    YES    NO**

# HOW TO USE – POSITIVE THOUGHTS

You can use POSITIVE THOUGHTS by considering your thoughts and asking yourself, "Is this thought POWERFUL? Is it PRODUCTIVE? Is it POSITIVE?"

When you ask yourself these three questions, you will become more in control of your thoughts.

THE THREE Ps
- Is it POWERFUL?   •   Is it PRODUCTIVE?   •   Is it POSITIVE?

If the answer is no, then pick a more POSITIVE THOUGHT.

# TELL US WHAT YOU JUST READ

You have just finished reading the POSITIVE THOUGHTS Basics. The Basics consist of the weeks you study POSITIVE THOUGHTS, the KEYWORDS, STATEMENT OF PURPOSE AND OWNERSHIP, OBJECTIVE, TOOL INTRO and HOW TO USE POSITIVE THOUGHTS. Remember ALL GOGI Tools were written *by* prisoners *for* prisoners.

*In your own words, explain the GOGI Tool POSITIVE THOUGHTS:*_____

_____
_____
_____
_____
_____
_____
_____
_____
_____
_____

# POSITIVE THOUGHTS Meeting

GOGI weeks begin on Monday. ONLY hold this meeting in the following weeks: (check the week you are studying the POSITIVE THOUGHTS Tool.)

❑2nd week of January   ❑2nd week of April   ❑ 2nd week of July   ❑ 2nd week of October

## Call Your Meeting to Order

*To be read by a volunteer:*

We call this GOGI meeting to order. We are gathered here today as a GOGI community of like-minded individuals who CLAIM RESPONSIBILITY for our lives in our own unique ways. We include the GOGI TOOLS FOR POSITIVE DECISION-MAKING as a supplement to our existing or potential spiritual and social support systems. We believe that the GOGI Tools help us on our journey toward internal freedom regardless of any perceived differences among us. We realize the GOGI TOOLS FOR POSITIVE DECISION-MAKING are learned according to a calendar and they are simple tools that may enhance many other practices that promote our health and well-being. We acknowledge the GOGI Tools as positive decision-making tools to help us in our daily living.

## The GOGI Purpose

*To be read by a volunteer:*

The purpose of GOGI is to provide simple tools to anyone interested in making more positive decisions in their lives. We do this through sharing the GOGI Tools which are taught in many ways and formats including independent-study, small group study, as well as formal educational programming offering course credit provided by institutions or educational organizations. Our purpose is to offer these tools as a positive and prosocial culture, not as a program, even in instances where GOGI is studied in a program format. We study the GOGI Tools according to the GOGI Calendar so no one will ever be alone in their study of GOGI. The GOGI Tools are to be shared freely among all people and should not be withheld for any reason.

## Reading of Your Tools *(To be read by a volunteer:)*

## The GOGI TOOLS FOR POSITIVE DECISION-MAKING are:

| | |
|---|---|
| BOSS OF MY BRAIN | CLAIM RESPONSIBILITY |
| BELLY BREATHING | LET GO |
| FIVE SECOND LIGHTSWITCH | FOR–GIVE |
| POSITIVE THOUGHTS | WHAT IF |
| POSITIVE WORDS | REALITY CHECK |
| POSITIVE ACTIONS | ULTIMATE FREEDOM |

## DAILY SIGN-IN – GROUP CERTIFICATE COURSE
### If you want to receive credit, please fill out the information below:

The month is _1_   The day of the month is _25_   The year is _20_   Signature _____

Meeting location_____   Start time _____   Number of people in my Group _____

**MY GROUP STUDIES ACCORDING TO THE GOGI CALENDAR (circle one)**   YES   NO

## This Week's Objective

*To be read by a volunteer:*
Your goal with this week's tool is to practice being the boss of your thinking and to choose thoughts that are POWERFUL, PRODUCTIVE, and POSITIVE. You will practice this with the tool POSITIVE THOUGHTS.

## Check in/Recap of Your Prior Week

A brief check in when group members share their progress with the tools.

## Your Group Discussion

Please have volunteers or preassigned group members read from any of the GOGI books. This can be anything from any of the GOGI books related to the tool of this week (according to the GOGI Calendar). You may wish to have multiple people read from different GOGI books.

## Your Group Questions and Activities

This is a perfect time to have an activity. Your group can discuss this tool and, if completing GOGI as a program for credit, now is a great time to review or have your group members complete any required written assignments.

## Close Your Meeting

*We invite you to join us for our next meeting to be held (date) where we will study the GOGI Tool: _____ (refer to Calendar). If we are unable to hold next week's meeting we will refer to the Calendar for the tool we will study at the next meeting. Course credit is earned by meeting twelve to fifteen times, even if tools are skipped or repeated.*

## GOGI Pledge

*To be read by a volunteer:*

*May our commitment (group repeat)*
*To the study of GOGI (group repeat)*
*Grant us the joy (group repeat)*
*Of giving and receiving (group repeat)*
*So that our inner freedom (group repeat)*
*May be of maximum service (group repeat)*
*To those we love (group repeat)*
*And infinite others (group repeat)*

*This art is a gift to GOGI from Keith E.*

## DAILY SIGN-IN – GROUP CERTIFICATE COURSE
**If you want to receive credit, please fill out the information below:**

The month is ___1___ The day of the month is _2 5_ The year is _20_ Signature _____

Meeting location_____ Start time _____ Number of people in my Group _____

**MY GROUP STUDIES ACCORDING TO THE GOGI CALENDAR (circle one)**    YES    NO

## Weekly Course Worksheet POSITIVE THOUGHTS

*In some situations, it is very difficult to remain positive...about anything. How can remembering the Three Ps – IS IT POWERFUL, IS IT PRODUCTIVE, and IS IT POSITIVE be helpful?*

_____

*Can you recall one time when POSITIVE THOUGHTS might have changed a situation? Briefly describe._____

_____*

*Having POSITIVE THOUGHTS can change your outcomes in life. Why do think that is true?_____*

_____

*Creating your own thoughts takes practice. If you practice throughout the day, what POSITIVE THOUGHTS would you create today?*

*1. I would think of: _____*

*2. I would also think of: _____*

*3. And I would think of: _____*

*Do you remember somebody in your past (a teacher, parent, grandparent, etc...) who always seemed to have POSITIVE THOUGHTS? How did you feel about that person at the time?*

_____

_____

*How do you look at that person now? _____*

_____

*How would you explain POSITIVE THOUGHTS to a young person? _____*

_____

_____

Deacon Joseph "Ice" P.
Corcoran, C
2013

*This art is a gift to GOGI from James H.*

# DAILY SIGN-IN – GROUP CERTIFICATE COURSE
**If you want to receive credit, please fill out the information below:**

The month is_____1_____ The day of the month is _25_ The year is _20_ Signature _____

Meeting location_____ Start time _____ Number of people in my Group _____

**MY GROUP STUDIES ACCORDING TO THE GOGI CALENDAR (circle one)   YES   NO**

## My GOGI Group Reflections

*In my GOGI Group this week I learned about the tool:* _____

_____

*This tool belongs to the section of tools called: The Tools of* _____

*I learned that this GOGI Tool has KEYWORDS. The KEYWORDS for this tool are:*

_____

_____

_____

*If I choose, I could apply this GOGI Tool to my daily life. Below is an example of how this tool might help me make better decisions:* _____

_____

_____

_____

*What I liked most about my GOGI Group this week was:* _____

_____

_____

*Meeting in a GOGI Group is helpful to my learning and growth because:* _____

_____

_____

*Here are some things I want to write down so that I do not forget them in the future. They are my thoughts and my observations about life and GOGI.* _____

_____

_____

_____

_____

# REMAIN ON THE GOGI CALENDAR

## Start the POSITIVE WORDS Meeting in 3 easy Steps

1. **Check the GOGI Calendar before your meeting**

2. **Read the GOGI Tools Basics before your meeting**

3. **Enjoy your GOGI Meeting**

# The GOGI POSITIVE WORDS Calendar
## For all GOGI meetings, remain on the GOGI calendar.

GOGI studies all tools according to the CALENDAR. GOGI weeks always start on Monday. Each month will start on Monday the 1st, 2nd, 3rd, 4th, 5th, 6th, or 7th. POSITIVE WORDS is studied by all GOGI students on the weeks circled below. Fifteen meetings makes one cycle of study. You might study one tool twice if a meeting was missed. That's okay!

### JANUARY
Week 1 BOSS OF MY BRAIN
Week 2 BELLY BREATHING
Week 3 FIVE SECOND LIGHTSWITCH
Week 4 POSITIVE THOUGHTS
Week 5 REVIEW ABOVE

### FEBRUARY
Week 1 POSITIVE WORDS
Week 2 POSITIVE ACTIONS
Week 3 CLAIM RESPONSIBILITY
Week 4 LET GO
Week 5 REVIEW ABOVE

### MARCH
Week 1 FOR-GIVE
Week 2 WHAT IF
Week 3 REALITY CHECK
Week 4 ULTIMATE FREEDOM
Week 5 REVIEW ABOVE

### APRIL
Week 1 BOSS OF MY BRAIN
Week 2 BELLY BREATHING
Week 3 FIVE SECOND LIGHTSWITCH
Week 4 POSITIVE THOUGHTS
Week 5 REVIEW ABOVE

### MAY
Week 1 POSITIVE WORDS
Week 2 POSITIVE ACTIONS
Week 3 CLAIM RESPONSIBILITY
Week 4 LET GO
Week 5 REVIEW ABOVE

### JUNE
Week 1 FOR-GIVE
Week 2 WHAT IF
Week 3 REALITY CHECK
Week 4 ULTIMATE FREEDOM
Week 5 REVIEW ABOVE

### JULY
Week 1 BOSS OF MY BRAIN
Week 2 BELLY BREATHING
Week 3 FIVE SECOND LIGHTSWITCH
Week 4 POSITIVE THOUGHTS
Week 5 REVIEW ABOVE

### AUGUST
Week 1 POSITIVE WORDS
Week 2 POSITIVE ACTIONS
Week 3 CLAIM RESPONSIBILITY
Week 4 LET GO
Week 5 REVIEW ABOVE

### SEPTEMBER
Week 1 FOR-GIVE
Week 2 WHAT IF
Week 3 REALITY CHECK
Week 4 ULTIMATE FREEDOM
Week 5 REVIEW ABOVE

### OCTOBER
Week 1 BOSS OF MY BRAIN
Week 2 BELLY BREATHING
Week 3 FIVE SECOND LIGHTSWITCH
Week 4 POSITIVE THOUGHTS
Week 5 REVIEW ABOVE

### NOVEMBER
Week 1 POSITIVE WORDS
Week 2 POSITIVE ACTIONS
Week 3 CLAIM RESPONSIBILITY
Week 4 LET GO
Week 5 REVIEW ABOVE

### DECEMBER
Week 1 FOR-GIVE
Week 2 WHAT IF
Week 3 REALITY CHECK
Week 4 ULTIMATE FREEDOM
Week 5 REVIEW ABOVE

# POSITIVE WORDS Basics

## Check the week you are holding this group study:

_____ 1st Week of February

_____ 1st Week of May

_____ 1st Week of August

_____ 1st Week of November

## KEYWORDS – POSITIVE WORDS

THE THREE Ps

Is it POWERFUL?  Is it PRODUCTIVE?  Is it POSITIVE?

## STATEMENT OF PURPOSE AND OWNERSHIP – POSITIVE WORDS

My POSITIVE WORDS tell the world what I am thinking and who I am today. I use POSITIVE WORDS to break free from my past and move forward into a positive future.

## OBJECTIVE – POSITIVE WORDS

Your goal this week is to practice being the boss of the words you choose. You will choose words that are POWERFUL, PRODUCTIVE, and POSITIVE when you learn the tool POSITIVE WORDS.

## TOOL INTRO – POSITIVE WORDS

Did you know that the words you choose tell the world quite a lot about you? Your words tell others what you are thinking, how you think, and if you are generally a positive or negative person.

POSITIVE WORDS have a powerful way of attracting POSITIVE ACTIONS. Getting in the habit of choosing more POSITIVE WORDS puts you in charge of how the world sees you and how you see yourself, which increases your POSITIVE ACTIONS automatically.

Negative words usually have the word "not" included in them. Words like "cannot" and "will not" and "could not" and "is not" are negative words. There are a bunch of other "not" words and they are negative words. Rather than picking a word with a "not" you can pick words that are POWERFUL, PRODUCTIVE, and POSITIVE.

## HOW TO USE – POSITIVE WORDS

You can use POSITIVE WORDS by asking yourself the THREE Ps. Are your words POWERFUL? Are they PRODUCTIVE? Are they POSITIVE? You can test to see if others are using POSITIVE WORDS by asking yourself if their words are POWERFUL, PRODUCTIVE, and POSITIVE.

Before you choose your words, test them out with the THREE Ps. Are your words POWERFUL? PRODUCTIVE? POSITIVE?

## TELL US WHAT YOU JUST READ

You have just finished reading the POSITIVE WORDS Basics. The Basics consist of the weeks you study POSITIVE WORDS, the KEYWORDS, STATEMENT OF PURPOSE AND OWNERSHIP, OBJECTIVE, TOOL INTRO and HOW TO USE POSITIVE WORDS. Remember ALL GOGI Tools were written *by* prisoners *for* prisoners.

*In your own words, explain the GOGI Tool POSITIVE WORDS:*_____

_____

_____

_____

_____

_____

_____

_____

**DAILY SIGN-IN – GROUP CERTIFICATE COURSE**
**If you want to receive credit, please fill out the information below:**
The month is ___Z___ The day of the month is ___l___ The year is ___70___ Signature _____
Meeting location_____ Start time _____ Number of people in my Group _____
MY GROUP STUDIES ACCORDING TO THE GOGI CALENDAR (circle one)   YES   NO

# POSITIVE WORDS Meeting

GOGI weeks begin on Monday. ONLY hold this meeting in the following weeks: (check the week you are studying the POSITIVE WORDS Tool.)

❑1st week of February   ❑1st week of May   ❑1st week of August   ❑ 1st week of November

## Call Your Meeting to Order

*To be read by a volunteer:*
We call this GOGI meeting to order. We are gathered here today as a GOGI community of like-minded individuals who CLAIM RESPONSIBILITY for our lives in our own unique ways. We include the GOGI TOOLS FOR POSITIVE DECISION-MAKING as a supplement to our existing or potential spiritual and social support systems. We believe that the GOGI Tools help us on our journey toward internal freedom regardless of any perceived differences among us. We realize the GOGI TOOLS FOR POSITIVE DECISION-MAKING are learned according to a calendar and they are simple tools that may enhance many other practices that promote our health and well-being. We acknowledge the GOGI Tools as positive decision-making tools to help us in our daily living.

## The GOGI Purpose

*To be read by a volunteer:*
The purpose of GOGI is to provide simple tools to anyone interested in making more positive decisions in their lives. We do this through sharing the GOGI Tools which are taught in many ways and formats including independent-study, small group study, as well as formal educational programming offering course credit provided by institutions or educational organizations. Our purpose is to offer these tools as a positive and prosocial culture, not as a program, even in instances where GOGI is studied in a program format. We study the GOGI Tools according to the GOGI Calendar so no one will ever be alone in their study of GOGI. The GOGI Tools are to be shared freely among all people and should not be withheld for any reason.

## Reading of Your Tools *(To be read by a volunteer:)*

## The GOGI TOOLS FOR POSITIVE DECISION-MAKING are:

| | |
|---|---|
| BOSS OF MY BRAIN | CLAIM RESPONSIBILITY |
| BELLY BREATHING | LET GO |
| FIVE SECOND LIGHTSWITCH | FOR–GIVE |
| POSITIVE THOUGHTS | WHAT IF |
| POSITIVE WORDS | REALITY CHECK |
| POSITIVE ACTIONS | ULTIMATE FREEDOM |

## DAILY SIGN-IN – GROUP CERTIFICATE COURSE
**If you want to receive credit, please fill out the information below:**

The month is ___2___ The day of the month is ___1___ The year is __20__ Signature _____

Meeting location _____ Start time _____ Number of people in my Group _____

**MY GROUP STUDIES ACCORDING TO THE GOGI CALENDAR (circle one)    YES    NO**

## This Week's Objective

*To be read by a volunteer:*
Your goal this week is to practice being the boss of the words you choose. You will choose words that are POWERFUL, PRODUCTIVE, and POSITIVE when we learn the tool POSITIVE WORDS.

## Check in/Recap of Your Prior Week

A brief check in when group members share their progress with the tools.

## Your Group Discussion

Please have volunteers or preassigned group members read from any of the GOGI books. This can be anything from any of the GOGI books related to the tool of this week (according to the GOGI Calendar). You may wish to have multiple people read from different GOGI books.

## Your Group Questions and Activities

This is a perfect time to have an activity. Your group can discuss this tool and, if completing GOGI as a program for credit, now is a great time to review or have your group members complete any required written assignments.

## Close Your Meeting

*We invite you to join us for our next meeting to be held (date) where we will study the GOGI Tool: _____ (refer to Calendar). If we are unable to hold next week's meeting we will refer to the Calendar for the tool we will study at the next meeting. Course credit is earned by meeting twelve to fifteen times, even if tools are skipped or repeated.*

## GOGI Pledge

*To be read by a volunteer:*

*May our commitment (group repeat)*
*To the study of GOGI (group repeat)*
*Grant us the joy (group repeat)*
*Of giving and receiving (group repeat)*
*So that our inner freedom (group repeat)*
*May be of maximum service (group repeat)*
*To those we love (group repeat)*
*And infinite others (group repeat)*

## DAILY SIGN-IN – GROUP CERTIFICATE COURSE
### If you want to receive credit, please fill out the information below:

The month is ___Z___ The day of the month is _____ The year is __Z O__ Signature _____
Meeting location_____ Start time _____ Number of people in my Group _____
**MY GROUP STUDIES ACCORDING TO THE GOGI CALENDAR (circle one)   YES   NO**

## Weekly Course Worksheet POSITIVE WORDS

*Many GOGI students come to understand the power of their words. Can you really hurt someone with words? Can POSITIVE WORDS have the opposite effect?* _____

_____

_____

*Write five of your favorite POSITIVE WORDS that are POWERFUL, PRODUCTIVE, and POSITIVE.*

1. _____
2. _____
3. _____
4. _____
5. _____

*What are three POSITIVE WORDS you would use when you describe yourself? I am:*

1. _____
2. _____
3. _____

*What were the last POSITIVE WORDS you said to someone else recently?* _____

_____

*If you were told to choose three POSITIVE WORDS to use regularly, what would those words be and why?*

1._____Why? _____
2._____Why? _____
3._____Why? _____

*When you were young, were there any POSITIVE WORDS that had an impact on you?* _____

_____

*Who said them to you and how did you feel?* _____

_____

# DAILY SIGN-IN – GROUP CERTIFICATE COURSE

**If you want to receive credit, please fill out the information below:**

The month is____*2*____ The day of the month is ____*1*____ The year is *2 0* Signature _____
Meeting location_____ Start time _____ Number of people in my Group _____
**MY GROUP STUDIES ACCORDING TO THE GOGI CALENDAR (circle one)   YES   NO**

## My GOGI Group Reflections

*In my GOGI Group this week I learned about the tool:* _____

_____

*This tool belongs to the section of tools called: The Tools of* _____

*I learned that this GOGI Tool has KEYWORDS. The KEYWORDS for this tool are:*

_____

_____

*If I choose, I could apply this GOGI Tool to my daily life. Below is an example of how this tool might help me make better decisions:* _____

_____

_____

_____

*What I liked most about my GOGI Group this week was:* _____

_____

_____

*Meeting in a GOGI Group is helpful to my learning and growth because:* _____

_____

_____

*Here are some things I want to write down so that I do not forget them in the future. They are my thoughts and my observations about life and GOGI.* _____

_____

_____

_____

_____

# REMAIN ON THE GOGI CALENDAR

## Start the POSITIVE ACTIONS
## Meeting in 3 easy Steps

1. **Check the GOGI Calendar before your meeting**

2. **Read the GOGI Tools Basics before your meeting**

3. **Enjoy your GOGI Meeting**

# The GOGI POSITIVE ACTIONS Calendar
## For all GOGI meetings, remain on the GOGI calendar.

GOGI studies all tools according to the CALENDAR. GOGI weeks always start on Monday. Each month will start on Monday the 1st, 2nd, 3rd, 4th, 5th, 6th, or 7th. POSITIVE ACTIONSis studied by all GOGI students on the weeks circled below. Fifteen meetings makes one cycle of study. You might study one tool twice if a meeting was missed. That's okay!

### JANUARY
Week 1 BOSS OF MY BRAIN
Week 2 BELLY BREATHING
Week 3 FIVE SECOND LIGHTSWITCH
Week 4 POSITIVE THOUGHTS
Week 5 REVIEW ABOVE

### FEBRUARY
Week 1 POSITIVE WORDS
Week 2 POSITIVE ACTIONS
Week 3 CLAIM RESPONSIBILITY
Week 4 LET GO
Week 5 REVIEW ABOVE

### MARCH
Week 1 FOR–GIVE
Week 2 WHAT IF
Week 3 REALITY CHECK
Week 4 ULTIMATE FREEDOM
Week 5 REVIEW ABOVE

### APRIL
Week 1 BOSS OF MY BRAIN
Week 2 BELLY BREATHING
Week 3 FIVE SECOND LIGHTSWITCH
Week 4 POSITIVE THOUGHTS
Week 5 REVIEW ABOVE

### MAY
Week 1 POSITIVE WORDS
Week 2 POSITIVE ACTIONS
Week 3 CLAIM RESPONSIBILITY
Week 4 LET GO
Week 5 REVIEW ABOVE

### JUNE
Week 1 FOR–GIVE
Week 2 WHAT IF
Week 3 REALITY CHECK
Week 4 ULTIMATE FREEDOM
Week 5 REVIEW ABOVE

### JULY
Week 1 BOSS OF MY BRAIN
Week 2 BELLY BREATHING
Week 3 FIVE SECOND LIGHTSWITCH
Week 4 POSITIVE THOUGHTS
Week 5 REVIEW ABOVE

### AUGUST
Week 1 POSITIVE WORDS
Week 2 POSITIVE ACTIONS
Week 3 CLAIM RESPONSIBILITY
Week 4 LET GO
Week 5 REVIEW ABOVE

### SEPTEMBER
Week 1 FOR–GIVE
Week 2 WHAT IF
Week 3 REALITY CHECK
Week 4 ULTIMATE FREEDOM
Week 5 REVIEW ABOVE

### OCTOBER
Week 1 BOSS OF MY BRAIN
Week 2 BELLY BREATHING
Week 3 FIVE SECOND LIGHTSWITCH
Week 4 POSITIVE THOUGHTS
Week 5 REVIEW ABOVE

### NOVEMBER
Week 1 POSITIVE WORDS
Week 2 POSITIVE ACTIONS
Week 3 CLAIM RESPONSIBILITY
Week 4 LET GO
Week 5 REVIEW ABOVE

### DECEMBER
Week 1 FOR–GIVE
Week 2 WHAT IF
Week 3 REALITY CHECK
Week 4 ULTIMATE FREEDOM
Week 5 REVIEW ABOVE

**DAILY SIGN-IN – GROUP CERTIFICATE COURSE**
If you want to receive credit, please fill out the information below:

The month is_____ The day of the month is _____The year is_____ Signature _____
Meeting location_____ Start time _____ Number of people in my Group _____
MY GROUP STUDIES ACCORDING TO THE GOGI CALENDAR (circle one)    YES    NO

# POSITIVE ACTIONS Basics

## Check the week you are holding this group study:

_____    2nd Week of February

_____    2nd Week of May

_____    2nd Week of August

_____    2nd Week of November

## KEYWORDS – POSITIVE ACTIONS

THE THREE Ps

Is it POWERFUL?  Is it PRODUCTIVE?  Is it POSITIVE?

## STATEMENT OF PURPOSE AND OWNERSHIP – POSITIVE ACTIONS

I know I have the power to transform my world through my POSITIVE ACTIONS.
I choose my POSITIVE ACTIONS so I can move beyond my past and create my
positive future.

## OBJECTIVE – POSITIVE ACTIONS

Your goal this week is to be the boss of all your actions.

You will choose actions that are POWERFUL, PRODUCTIVE, and POSITIVE when
you learn the tool POSITIVE ACTIONS.

## TOOL INTRO – POSITIVE ACTIONS

Did you know that just doing one small POSITIVE ACTION may have a big positive
result in your day? Yes, that is correct, even one small POSITIVE ACTION each day
can help you a great deal in your ability to be the boss of your life.

POSITIVE ACTIONS are the small things you do, not necessarily the big things. The
smaller POSITIVE ACTIONS are actually more powerful, because you can do more
of them each day.

Did you know that if you have two to three POSITIVE ACTIONS picked out ahead of time, it is easier to overcome urges to make a poor decision?

## HOW TO USE – POSITIVE ACTIONS

When you pick out two or three POSITIVE ACTIONS you will have them ready for your thought process. Having POSITIVE ACTIONS ready is important, because you may need to use them when the urge to make a poor choice seems to be pulling at you. Get your POSITIVE ACTIONS ready. Have them waiting.

Some examples of POSITIVE ACTIONS are: having a glass of water, walking around the block, exercising, picking up a good book, calling a sponsor or church friend, or cleaning up your living space.

## TELL US WHAT YOU JUST READ

You have just finished reading the POSITIVE ACTIONS Basics. The Basics consist of the weeks you study POSITIVE ACTIONS, the KEYWORDS, STATEMENT OF PURPOSE AND OWNERSHIP, OBJECTIVE, TOOL INTRO and HOW TO USE POSITIVE ACTIONS. Remember ALL GOGI Tools were written **by** prisoners **for** prisoners.

*In your own words, explain the GOGI Tool POSITIVE ACTIONS:*_____

_____

_____

_____

_____

_____

_____

_____

_____

# POSITIVE ACTIONS Meeting

GOGI weeks begin on Monday. ONLY hold this meeting in the following weeks: (check the week you are studying the POSITIVE ACTIONS Tool.)

❏2nd Week of February   ❏2nd Week of August   ❏2nd Week of May   ❏2nd Week of November

## Call Your Meeting to Order

*To be read by a volunteer:*
We call this GOGI meeting to order. We are gathered here today as a GOGI community of like-minded individuals who CLAIM RESPONSIBILITY for our lives in our own unique ways. We include the GOGI TOOLS FOR POSITIVE DECISION-MAKING as a supplement to our existing or potential spiritual and social support systems. We believe that the GOGI Tools help us on our journey toward internal freedom regardless of any perceived differences among us. We realize the GOGI TOOLS FOR POSITIVE DECISION-MAKING are learned according to a calendar and they are simple tools that may enhance many other practices that promote our health and well-being. We acknowledge the GOGI Tools as positive decision-making tools to help us in our daily living.

## The GOGI Purpose

*To be read by a volunteer:*
The purpose of GOGI is to provide simple tools to anyone interested in making more positive decisions in their lives. We do this through sharing the GOGI Tools which are taught in many ways and formats including independent-study, small group study, as well as formal educational programming offering course credit provided by institutions or educational organizations. Our purpose is to offer these tools as a positive and prosocial culture, not as a program, even in instances where GOGI is studied in a program format. We study the GOGI Tools according to the GOGI Calendar so no one will ever be alone in their study of GOGI. The GOGI Tools are to be shared freely among all people and should not be withheld for any reason.

## Reading of Your Tools *(To be read by a volunteer:)*

# The GOGI TOOLS FOR POSITIVE DECISION-MAKING are:

| | |
|---|---|
| BOSS OF MY BRAIN | CLAIM RESPONSIBILITY |
| BELLY BREATHING | LET GO |
| FIVE SECOND LIGHTSWITCH | FOR–GIVE |
| POSITIVE THOUGHTS | WHAT IF |
| POSITIVE WORDS | REALITY CHECK |
| POSITIVE ACTIONS | ULTIMATE FREEDOM |

## DAILY SIGN-IN – GROUP CERTIFICATE COURSE
### If you want to receive credit, please fill out the information below:

The month is_____ The day of the month is _____The year is_____ Signature _____

Meeting location_____ Start time _____ Number of people in my Group _____

**MY GROUP STUDIES ACCORDING TO THE GOGI CALENDAR (circle one)   YES   NO**

## This Week's Objective

*To be read by a volunteer:*
Your goal this week is to be the boss of all your actions. You will choose actions that are POWERFUL, PRODUCTIVE, and POSITIVE when you learn the tool POSITIVE ACTIONS.

## Check in/Recap of Your Prior Week

A brief check in when group members share their progress with the tools.

## Your Group Discussion

Please have volunteers or preassigned group members read from any of the GOGI books. This can be anything from any of the GOGI books related to the tool of this week (according to the GOGI Calendar). You may wish to have multiple people read from different GOGI books.

## Your Group Questions and Activities

This is a perfect time to have an activity. Your group can discuss this tool and, if completing GOGI as a program for credit, now is a great time to review or have your group members complete any required written assignments.

## Close Your Meeting

*We invite you to join us for our next meeting to be held (date) where we will study the GOGI Tool: _____ (refer to Calendar). If we are unable to hold next week's meeting we will refer to the Calendar for the tool we will study at the next meeting. Course credit is earned by meeting twelve to fifteen times, even if tools are skipped or repeated.*

## GOGI Pledge

*To be read by a volunteer:*

*May our commitment (group repeat)*
*To the study of GOGI (group repeat)*
*Grant us the joy (group repeat)*
*Of giving and receiving (group repeat)*
*So that our inner freedom (group repeat)*
*May be of maximum service (group repeat)*
*To those we love (group repeat)*
*And infinite others (group repeat)*

## My Gitt to GOGI ~ my art, poem or activity

My signature *Diego Huerta*

Print your name DIEGO.HUERTA

ID number _____ Location _____

*This art is a gift to GOGI from Oso.*

## DAILY SIGN-IN – GROUP CERTIFICATE COURSE
### If you want to receive credit, please fill out the information below:

The month is_____ The day of the month is _____ The year is_____ Signature _____

Meeting location_____ Start time _____ Number of people in my Group _____

MY GROUP STUDIES ACCORDING TO THE GOGI CALENDAR (circle one)    YES    NO

## Weekly Course Worksheet POSITIVE ACTIONS

*If you were asked to have three POSITIVE ACTIONS ready for when you're not feeling positive, what could they be?*

*1. My action would be to:* _____

*2. Another option would be:* _____

*3. Or, I could always:* _____

*Many GOGI students say that POSITIVE ACTIONS can help you move beyond your past and create a more positive future. Do you agree? Why or why not?* _____

_____

_____

*GOGI students often say they were once impulsive, angry or addicted. If you had used POSITIVE ACTIONS five, ten, or fifteen years ago, would your current life be different? How?*

_____

_____

*You've learned POSITIVE ACTIONS this week, how does this work with other GOGI Tools you've learned? List three below and how they work together.*

*1. POSITIVE ACTIONS work with BOSS OF MY BRAIN because:* _____

_____

_____

*2. POSITIVE ACTIONS works with BELLY BREATHING because:* _____

_____

_____

*3. POSITIVE ACTIONS works with FIVE SECOND LIGHTSWITCH because:*_____

_____

_____

Print your name <u>DONALD E. BROOKS</u> Sr

# DAILY SIGN-IN – GROUP CERTIFICATE COURSE
### If you want to receive credit, please fill out the information below:

The month is_____ The day of the month is _____ The year is_____ Signature _____
Meeting location_____ Start time _____ Number of people in my Group _____
**MY GROUP STUDIES ACCORDING TO THE GOGI CALENDAR (circle one)     YES     NO**

## My GOGI Group Reflections

*In my GOGI Group this week I learned about the tool:* _____

_____

*This tool belongs to the section of tools called: The Tools of* _____

*I learned that this GOGI Tool has KEYWORDS. The KEYWORDS for this tool are:*

_____

_____

_____

*If I choose, I could apply this GOGI Tool to my daily life. Below is an example of how this tool might help me make better decisions:*_____

_____

_____

_____

*What I liked most about my GOGI Group this week was:* _____

_____

_____

*Meeting in a GOGI Group is helpful to my learning and growth because:* _____

_____

_____

*Here are some things I want to write down so that I do not forget them in the future. They are my thoughts and my observations about life and GOGI.* _____

_____

_____

_____

_____

# REMAIN ON THE

# GOGI

# CALENDAR

## LOCKDOWN?

Did you miss any weeks due to lockdown or inability to meet?

## STAY ON CALENDAR!!!!

It means you WILL repeat a tool or two.

## That is OK.

On the following pages are BLANK MEETING FORMS for you to complete. You will repeat a tool, if a meeting is not held. That is OK. You will remain on calendar and do that tool twice. No sweat. Want to study ALL the GOGI Tools? We guess that means you are just going to need to sign up for another round of GOGI, right?

## STAY ON CALENDAR!

## DAILY SIGN-IN – GROUP CERTIFICATE COURSE
**If you want to receive credit, please fill out the information below:**

The month is_____ The day of the month is _____ The year is_____ Signature _____

Meeting location_____ Start time _____ Number of people in my Group _____

MY GROUP STUDIES ACCORDING TO THE GOGI CALENDAR (circle one)     YES     NO

## Blank Weekly Course Worksheet

Date:_____

The GOGI Tool of the week is (see the GOGI Calendar in this book): _____

_____

Write the KEYWORDS for this week's tool: _____

_____

_____

What did you like most about this week's meeting?  _____

_____

_____

How do GOGI meetings help you in your efforts to make more positive decisions?

_____

_____

_____

Give two examples of how you think you could use this particular tool your daily life:

_____

_____

How would you explain this tool to a friend not acquainted with GOGI?

_____

_____

_____

Finish this sentence: This week's tool will help me... _____

_____

## DAILY SIGN-IN – GROUP CERTIFICATE COURSE
**If you want to receive credit, please fill out the information below:**

The month is_____ The day of the month is _____The year is_____ Signature _____
Meeting location_____ Start time _____ Number of people in my Group _____
MY GROUP STUDIES ACCORDING TO THE GOGI CALENDAR (circle one)　　YES　　NO

## Blank Weekly Course Worksheet

Date:_____

The GOGI Tool of the week is (see the GOGI Calendar in this book): _____

_____

Write the KEYWORDS for this week's tool: _____

_____

_____

What did you like most about this week's meeting? _____

_____

_____

How do GOGI meetings help you in your efforts to make more positive decisions?

_____

_____

_____

Give two examples of how you think you could use this particular tool your daily life:

_____

_____

How would you explain this tool to a friend not acquainted with GOGI?

_____

_____

_____

Finish this sentence: This week's tool will help me... _____

_____

## DAILY SIGN-IN – GROUP CERTIFICATE COURSE
### If you want to receive credit, please fill out the information below:

The month is_____ The day of the month is _____ The year is_____ Signature _____

Meeting location_____ Start time _____ Number of people in my Group _____

MY GROUP STUDIES ACCORDING TO THE GOGI CALENDAR (circle one)   YES   NO

*This is the second week that you studied this tool. What is different about this week's study? What did you learn that you did not learn in the first week of study?* _____

_____

_____

_____

_____

*There are GOGI students who study the tools on calendar week after week, month after month, and year after year. In your opinion, what is the benefit of taking a second and third look at this particular tool?* _____

_____

_____

_____

*Most GOGI students believe that it is better to master ONE tool than to get to know all the tools just a little. As you get to know this week's tool more intensely, what is your opinion about "mastery" of the tool?* _____

_____

_____

*If you were assigned to teach someone this tool, what do you think are the most important aspects of this tool that you would teach?*

_____

_____

_____

_____

_____

_____

## DAILY SIGN-IN – GROUP CERTIFICATE COURSE
**If you want to receive credit, please fill out the information below:**

The month is_____ The day of the month is _____ The year is_____ Signature _____

Meeting location_____ Start time _____ Number of people in my Group _____

**MY GROUP STUDIES ACCORDING TO THE GOGI CALENDAR (circle one)     YES     NO**

## Blank Weekly Course Worksheet

Date:_____

The GOGI Tool of the week is (see the GOGI Calendar in this book): _____

_____

Write the KEYWORDS for this week's tool: _____

_____

_____

What did you like most about this week's meeting?  _____

_____

_____

How do GOGI meetings help you in your efforts to make more positive decisions?

_____

_____

_____

Give two examples of how you think you could use this particular tool your daily life:

_____

_____

How would you explain this tool to a friend not acquainted with GOGI?

_____

_____

_____

Finish this sentence: This week's tool will help me... _____

_____

# DAILY SIGN-IN – GROUP CERTIFICATE COURSE
## If you want to receive credit, please fill out the information below:

The month is_____ The day of the month is _____ The year is_____ Signature _____

Meeting location_____ Start time _____ Number of people in my Group _____

**MY GROUP STUDIES ACCORDING TO THE GOGI CALENDAR (circle one)    YES    NO**

*This is the second week that you studied this tool. What is different about this week's study? What did you learn that you did not learn in the first week of study?* _____

_____

_____

_____

_____

*There are GOGI students who study the tools on calendar week after week, month after month, and year after year. In your opinion, what is the benefit of taking a second and third look at this particular tool?* _____

_____

_____

_____

*Most GOGI students believe that it is better to master ONE tool than to get to know all the tools just a little. As you get to know this week's tool more intensely, what is your opinion about "mastery" of the tool?* _____

_____

_____

*If you were assigned to teach someone this tool, what do you think are the most important aspects of this tool that you would teach?*

_____

_____

_____

_____

_____

_____

_____

## DAILY SIGN-IN – GROUP CERTIFICATE COURSE

**If you want to receive credit, please fill out the information below:**

The month is_____ The day of the month is _____ The year is_____ Signature _____

Meeting location_____ Start time _____ Number of people in my Group _____

**MY GROUP STUDIES ACCORDING TO THE GOGI CALENDAR (circle one)    YES    NO**

## Blank Weekly Course Worksheet

Date:_____

The GOGI Tool of the week is (see the GOGI Calendar in this book): _____

_____

Write the KEYWORDS for this week's tool: _____

_____

_____

What did you like most about this week's meeting?  _____

_____

_____

How do GOGI meetings help you in your efforts to make more positive decisions?

_____

_____

_____

Give two examples of how you think you could use this particular tool your daily life:

_____

_____

How would you explain this tool to a friend not acquainted with GOGI?

_____

_____

_____

Finish this sentence: This week's tool will help me... _____

_____

## DAILY SIGN-IN – GROUP CERTIFICATE COURSE
### If you want to receive credit, please fill out the information below:

The month is_____ The day of the month is _____The year is_____ Signature _____

Meeting location_____ Start time _____ Number of people in my Group _____

**MY GROUP STUDIES ACCORDING TO THE GOGI CALENDAR (circle one)     YES     NO**

*This is the second week that you studied this tool. What is different about this week's study? What did you learn that you did not learn in the first week of study?* _____

_____

_____

_____

_____

*There are GOGI students who study the tools on calendar week after week, month after month, and year after year. In your opinion, what is the benefit of taking a second and third look at this particular tool?* _____

_____

_____

_____

*Most GOGI students believe that it is better to master ONE tool than to get to know all the tools just a little. As you get to know this week's tool more intensely, what is your opinion about "mastery" of the tool?* _____

_____

_____

*If you were assigned to teach someone this tool, what do you think are the most important aspects of this tool that you would teach?*

_____

_____

_____

_____

_____

_____

_____

# REMAIN ON THE GOGI CALENDAR

## Start the CLAIM RESPONSIBILITY Meeting in 3 easy Steps

1. Check the **GOGI** Calendar before your meeting

2. Read the **GOGI** Tools Basics before your meeting

3. Enjoy your **GOGI** Meeting

# The GOGI CLAIM RESPONSIBILITY Calendar
## For all GOGI meetings, remain on the GOGI calendar.

GOGI studies all tools according to the CALENDAR. GOGI weeks always start on Monday. Each month will start on Monday the 1st, 2nd, 3rd, 4th, 5th, 6th, or 7th. CLAIM RESPONSIBILITY is studied by all GOGI students on the weeks circled below. Fifteen meetings makes one cycle of study. You might study one tool twice if a meeting was missed. That's okay!

### JANUARY
Week 1 BOSS OF MY BRAIN
Week 2 BELLY BREATHING
Week 3 FIVE SECOND LIGHTSWITCH
Week 4 POSITIVE THOUGHTS
Week 5 REVIEW ABOVE

### FEBRUARY
Week 1 POSITIVE WORDS
Week 2 POSITIVE ACTIONS
Week 3 CLAIM RESPONSIBILITY
Week 4 LET GO
Week 5 REVIEW ABOVE

### MARCH
Week 1 FOR-GIVE
Week 2 WHAT IF
Week 3 REALITY CHECK
Week 4 ULTIMATE FREEDOM
Week 5 REVIEW ABOVE

### APRIL
Week 1 BOSS OF MY BRAIN
Week 2 BELLY BREATHING
Week 3 FIVE SECOND LIGHTSWITCH
Week 4 POSITIVE THOUGHTS
Week 5 REVIEW ABOVE

### MAY
Week 1 POSITIVE WORDS
Week 2 POSITIVE ACTIONS
Week 3 CLAIM RESPONSIBILITY
Week 4 LET GO
Week 5 REVIEW ABOVE

### JUNE
Week 1 FOR-GIVE
Week 2 WHAT IF
Week 3 REALITY CHECK
Week 4 ULTIMATE FREEDOM
Week 5 REVIEW ABOVE

### JULY
Week 1 BOSS OF MY BRAIN
Week 2 BELLY BREATHING
Week 3 FIVE SECOND LIGHTSWITCH
Week 4 POSITIVE THOUGHTS
Week 5 REVIEW ABOVE

### AUGUST
Week 1 POSITIVE WORDS
Week 2 POSITIVE ACTIONS
Week 3 CLAIM RESPONSIBILITY
Week 4 LET GO
Week 5 REVIEW ABOVE

### SEPTEMBER
Week 1 FOR-GIVE
Week 2 WHAT IF
Week 3 REALITY CHECK
Week 4 ULTIMATE FREEDOM
Week 5 REVIEW ABOVE

### OCTOBER
Week 1 BOSS OF MY BRAIN
Week 2 BELLY BREATHING
Week 3 FIVE SECOND LIGHTSWITCH
Week 4 POSITIVE THOUGHTS
Week 5 REVIEW ABOVE

### NOVEMBER
Week 1 POSITIVE WORDS
Week 2 POSITIVE ACTIONS
Week 3 CLAIM RESPONSIBILITY
Week 4 LET GO
Week 5 REVIEW ABOVE

### DECEMBER
Week 1 FOR-GIVE
Week 2 WHAT IF
Week 3 REALITY CHECK
Week 4 ULTIMATE FREEDOM
Week 5 REVIEW ABOVE

## DAILY SIGN-IN – GROUP CERTIFICATE COURSE
If you want to receive credit, please fill out the information below:

The month is_____ The day of the month is _____ The year is_____ Signature _____
Meeting location_____ Start time _____ Number of people in my Group _____
MY GROUP STUDIES ACCORDING TO THE GOGI CALENDAR (circle one)     YES     NO

# CLAIM RESPONSIBILITY Basics

## Check the week you are holding this group study:

_____ 3rd Week of February

_____ 3rd Week of May

_____ 3rd Week of August

_____ 3rd Week of November

## KEYWORDS – CLAIM RESPONSIBILITY

AM I PROUD OF THIS CHOICE?

I am responsible for all my actions and all my reactions today.

## STATEMENT OF PURPOSE AND OWNERSHIP – CLAIM RESPONSIBILITY

From this moment forward, I CLAIM RESPONSIBILITY for all my actions and all my reactions. All my actions and my reactions today are my responsibility and I CLAIM RESPONSIBILITY.

## OBJECTIVE – CLAIM RESPONSIBILITY

This week you get to learn that the tool CLAIM RESPONSIBILITY puts you in charge of your reactions and actions today. CLAIM RESPONSIBILITY permits you to be the boss of how you handle problems and circumstances today.

## TOOL INTRO – CLAIM RESPONSIBILITY

CLAIM RESPONSIBILITY allows you to focus on today. You do not need to focus on yesterday and you do not need to focus on tomorrow. With CLAIM RESPONSIBILITY you focus on today.

CLAIM RESPONSIBILITY lets you be the boss of your actions and of your reactions today. How you act today and how you react today is your decision. You are the boss.

**DAILY SIGN-IN – GROUP CERTIFICATE COURSE**
**If you want to receive credit, please fill out the information below:**

The month is_____ The day of the month is _____The year is_____ Signature _____
Meeting location_____ Start time _____ Number of people in my Group _____
**MY GROUP STUDIES ACCORDING TO THE GOGI CALENDAR (circle one)    YES     NO**

## HOW TO USE – CLAIM RESPONSIBILITY?

CLAIM RESPONSIBILITY is your power tool to help you control your actions and your reactions today. As a tool, CLAIM RESPONSIBILITY is not about the past, it is about your actions and reactions today.

You use CLAIM RESPONSIBILITY during the day when something happens or someone does something that would usually upset or concern you. With CLAIM RESPONSIBILITY you are being the boss of how you handle these situations.

Simply state: "Today I CLAIM RESPONSIBILITY for my actions and today I CLAIM RESPONSIBILITY for my reactions."

## TELL US WHAT YOU JUST READ

You have just finished reading the CLAIM RESPONSIBILITY Basics. The Basics consist of the weeks you study CLAIM RESPONSIBILITY, the KEYWORDS, STATEMENT OF PURPOSE AND OWNERSHIP, OBJECTIVE, TOOL INTRO and HOW TO USE CLAIM RESPONSIBILITY. Remember ALL GOGI Tools were written *by* prisoners *for* prisoners.

*In your own words, explain the GOGI Tool CLAIM RESPONSIBILITY:*_____

_____

_____

_____

_____

_____

_____

_____

_____

_____

# CLAIM RESPONSIBILITY Meeting

GOGI weeks begin on Monday. ONLY hold this meeting in the following weeks: (check the week you are studying the CLAIM RESPONSIBILITY Tool.)

❑3rd Week of February    ❑3rd Week of August    ❑ 3rd Week of May    ❑3rd Week of November

## Call Your Meeting to Order

*To be read by a volunteer:*

We call this GOGI meeting to order. We are gathered here today as a GOGI community of like-minded individuals who CLAIM RESPONSIBILITY for our lives in our own unique ways. We include the GOGI TOOLS FOR POSITIVE DECISION-MAKING as a supplement to our existing or potential spiritual and social support systems. We believe that the GOGI Tools help us on our journey toward internal freedom regardless of any perceived differences among us. We realize the GOGI TOOLS FOR POSITIVE DECISION-MAKING are learned according to a calendar and they are simple tools that may enhance many other practices that promote our health and well-being. We acknowledge the GOGI Tools as positive decision-making tools to help us in our daily living.

## The GOGI Purpose

*To be read by a volunteer:*

The purpose of GOGI is to provide simple tools to anyone interested in making more positive decisions in their lives. We do this through sharing the GOGI Tools which are taught in many ways and formats including independent-study, small group study, as well as formal educational programming offering course credit provided by institutions or educational organizations. Our purpose is to offer these tools as a positive and prosocial culture, not as a program, even in instances where GOGI is studied in a program format. We study the GOGI Tools according to the GOGI Calendar so no one will ever be alone in their study of GOGI. The GOGI Tools are to be shared freely among all people and should not be withheld for any reason.

## Reading of Your Tools *(To be read by a volunteer:)*

## The GOGI TOOLS FOR POSITIVE DECISION-MAKING are:

| | |
|---|---|
| BOSS OF MY BRAIN | CLAIM RESPONSIBILITY |
| BELLY BREATHING | LET GO |
| FIVE SECOND LIGHTSWITCH | FOR–GIVE |
| POSITIVE THOUGHTS | WHAT IF |
| POSITIVE WORDS | REALITY CHECK |
| POSITIVE ACTIONS | ULTIMATE FREEDOM |

## DAILY SIGN-IN – GROUP CERTIFICATE COURSE
### If you want to receive credit, please fill out the information below:

The month is_____ The day of the month is _____ The year is_____ Signature _____

Meeting location_____ Start time _____ Number of people in my Group _____

**MY GROUP STUDIES ACCORDING TO THE GOGI CALENDAR (circle one)    YES    NO**

## This Week's Objective

*To be read by a volunteer:*

This week you get to learn that the tool CLAIM RESPONSIBILITY puts you in charge of your reactions and actions today. CLAIM RESPONSIBILITY permits you to be the boss of how you handle problems and circumstances today.

## Check in/Recap of Your Prior Week

A brief check in when group members share their progress with the tools.

## Your Group Discussion

Please have volunteers or preassigned group members read from any of the GOGI books. This can be anything from any of the GOGI books related to the tool of this week (according to the GOGI Calendar). You may wish to have multiple people read from different GOGI books.

## Your Group Questions and Activities

This is a perfect time to have an activity. Your group can discuss this tool and, if completing GOGI as a program for credit, now is a great time to review or have your group members complete any required written assignments.

## Close Your Meeting

*We invite you to join us for our next meeting to be held (date) where we will study the GOGI Tool: _____ (refer to Calendar). If we are unable to hold next week's meeting we will refer to the Calendar for the tool we will study at the next meeting. Course credit is earned by meeting twelve to fifteen times, even if tools are skipped or repeated.*

## GOGI Pledge

*To be read by a volunteer:*

*May our commitment (group repeat)*
*To the study of GOGI (group repeat)*
*Grant us the joy (group repeat)*
*Of giving and receiving (group repeat)*
*So that our inner freedom (group repeat)*
*May be of maximum service (group repeat)*
*To those we love (group repeat)*
*And infinite others (group repeat)*

*This art is a gift to GOGI from Vinson.*

## DAILY SIGN-IN – GROUP CERTIFICATE COURSE
**If you want to receive credit, please fill out the information below:**

The month is_____ The day of the month is _____ The year is_____ Signature _____

Meeting location_____ Start time _____ Number of people in my Group _____

**MY GROUP STUDIES ACCORDING TO THE GOGI CALENDAR (circle one)    YES    NO**

## Weekly Course Worksheet CLAIM RESPONSIBILITY

*It is very easy to say 'not my fault' or 'it wasn't me.' Why is it harder to CLAIM RESPONSIBILITY for your actions and reactions?* _____

_____

_____

*What is one choice you are proud of in your life? Why are you proud of that choice?_*

_____

_____

*Some GOGI students state that it is difficult to acknowledge positive choices. Why might it be difficult for some people to see the positive?* _____

_____

_____

_____

*Using the tool CLAIM RESPONSIBILITY is not only about being proud of your choices, it's also about being responsible for your actions and reactions to other peoples' choices that affect you. Why do you think that is important?* _____

_____

_____

_____

*How could the tool CLAIM RESPONSIBILITY have an impact on your friendships?*

_____

*Your family?* _____

_____

*Your work?* _____

_____

*Your freedom?* _____

_____

Everything Branches out from the Root of GOGI

BOSS OF MY BRAIN

BELLY BREATHING

FIVE SECOND LIGHT SWITCH

POSITIVE THOUGHTS, WORDS, & ACTIONS

CLAIM RESPONSIBILITY

LET GO

FORGIVE

REALITY CHECK

ULTIMATE FREEDOM

*This art is a gift from New York GOGI student Jose LaFontaine.*

## DAILY SIGN-IN – GROUP CERTIFICATE COURSE
### If you want to receive credit, please fill out the information below:

The month is_____ The day of the month is _____ The year is_____ Signature _____

Meeting location_____ Start time _____ Number of people in my Group _____

**MY GROUP STUDIES ACCORDING TO THE GOGI CALENDAR (circle one)    YES    NO**

## My GOGI Group Reflections

*GOGI studies according to the GOGI Calendar. Look at the calendar. Did your group remain on calendar this week? Yes or No* _____

*In my GOGI Group this week I learned about the tool:* _____

*This tool belongs to the section of tools called: The Tools of* _____

*I learned that this GOGI Tool has KEYWORDS. The KEYWORDS for this tool are:*

_____

_____

_____

_____

*If I choose, I could apply this GOGI Tool to my daily life. Below is an example of how this tool might help me make better decisions:*_____

_____

_____

_____

*What I liked most about my GOGI Group this week was:* _____

_____

_____

*Meeting in a GOGI Group is helpful to my learning and growth because:* _____

_____

_____

*Here are some things I want to write down so that I do not forget them in the future. They are my thoughts and my observations about life and GOGI.* _____

_____

_____

# REMAIN ON THE GOGI CALENDAR

## Start the LET GO

## Meeting in 3 easy Steps

1. **Check the GOGI Calendar before your meeting**

2. **Read the GOGI Tools Basics before your meeting**

3. **Enjoy your GOGI Meeting**

# The GOGI LET GO Calendar
## For all GOGI meetings, remain on the GOGI calendar.

GOGI studies all tools according to the CALENDAR. GOGI weeks always start on Monday. Each month will start on Monday the 1st, 2nd, 3rd, 4th, 5th, 6th, or 7th. LET GO is studied by all GOGI students on the weeks circled below. Fifteen meetings makes one cycle of study.
You might study one tool twice if a meeting was missed. That's okay!

### JANUARY
Week 1 BOSS OF MY BRAIN
Week 2 BELLY BREATHING
Week 3 FIVE SECOND LIGHTSWITCH
Week 4 POSITIVE THOUGHTS
Week 5 REVIEW ABOVE

### FEBRUARY
Week 1 POSITIVE WORDS
Week 2 POSITIVE ACTIONS
Week 3 CLAIM RESPONSIBILITY
Week 4 LET GO
Week 5 REVIEW ABOVE

### MARCH
Week 1 FOR-GIVE
Week 2 WHAT IF
Week 3 REALITY CHECK
Week 4 ULTIMATE FREEDOM
Week 5 REVIEW ABOVE

### APRIL
Week 1 BOSS OF MY BRAIN
Week 2 BELLY BREATHING
Week 3 FIVE SECOND LIGHTSWITCH
Week 4 POSITIVE THOUGHTS
Week 5 REVIEW ABOVE

### MAY
Week 1 POSITIVE WORDS
Week 2 POSITIVE ACTIONS
Week 3 CLAIM RESPONSIBILITY
Week 4 LET GO
Week 5 REVIEW ABOVE

### JUNE
Week 1 FOR-GIVE
Week 2 WHAT IF
Week 3 REALITY CHECK
Week 4 ULTIMATE FREEDOM
Week 5 REVIEW ABOVE

### JULY
Week 1 BOSS OF MY BRAIN
Week 2 BELLY BREATHING
Week 3 FIVE SECOND LIGHTSWITCH
Week 4 POSITIVE THOUGHTS
Week 5 REVIEW ABOVE

### AUGUST
Week 1 POSITIVE WORDS
Week 2 POSITIVE ACTIONS
Week 3 CLAIM RESPONSIBILITY
Week 4 LET GO
Week 5 REVIEW ABOVE

### SEPTEMBER
Week 1 FOR-GIVE
Week 2 WHAT IF
Week 3 REALITY CHECK
Week 4 ULTIMATE FREEDOM
Week 5 REVIEW ABOVE

### OCTOBER
Week 1 BOSS OF MY BRAIN
Week 2 BELLY BREATHING
Week 3 FIVE SECOND LIGHTSWITCH
Week 4 POSITIVE THOUGHTS
Week 5 REVIEW ABOVE

### NOVEMBER
Week 1 POSITIVE WORDS
Week 2 POSITIVE ACTIONS
Week 3 CLAIM RESPONSIBILITY
Week 4 LET GO
Week 5 REVIEW ABOVE

### DECEMBER
Week 1 FOR-GIVE
Week 2 WHAT IF
Week 3 REALITY CHECK
Week 4 ULTIMATE FREEDOM
Week 5 REVIEW ABOVE

**DAILY SIGN-IN – GROUP CERTIFICATE COURSE**
If you want to receive credit, please fill out the information below:

The month is_____ The day of the month is _____ The year is_____ Signature _____
Meeting location_____ Start time _____ Number of people in my Group _____
MY GROUP STUDIES ACCORDING TO THE GOGI CALENDAR (circle one)   YES    NO

# LET GO Basics

## Check the week you are holding this group study:

_____ 4th Week of February

_____ 4th Week of May

_____ 4th Week of August

_____ 4th Week of November

## KEYWORDS – LET GO

HAND/SQUASH/TOSS:
When bothered, I put the feeling in my hand, squash it, and toss it away from me.

## STATEMENT OF PURPOSE AND OWNERSHIP – LET GO

The best way to focus on living in the present and moving forward is if I LET GO of anything which has held me back. When I LET GO, I move forward and I set myself free.

## OBJECTIVE – LET GO

Your goal this week is to practice the power of putting problems in your HAND, then SQUASH them and TOSS them away. This tool, called LET GO, will permit you to HAND/SQUASH/TOSS anything that might stand in your way.

## TOOL INTRO – LET GO

GOGI knows there are things in your past that might seem too big to ever move beyond. Sometimes it seems as if the bad stuff has controlled and defined your life. That is sometimes a normal way to feel.

You can use the GOGI TOOL called LET GO for the big things, but also for the daily little things. You can begin to use this tool to get past the daily irritations that happen to everyone.

**DAILY SIGN-IN – GROUP CERTIFICATE COURSE**
**If you want to receive credit, please fill out the information below:**

The month is_____ The day of the month is _____ The year is_____ Signature _____

Meeting location_____ Start time _____ Number of people in my Group _____

**MY GROUP STUDIES ACCORDING TO THE GOGI CALENDAR (circle one)     YES     NO**

## HOW TO USE – LET GO

You use LET GO for the daily irritations, those things that seem to creep up on you and try to trip you up. Someone bumps into you? Give it the LET GO - HAND/SQUASH/TOSS. Didn't get that job? Give it the LET GO. Didn't like how someone spoke to you? Give it the LET GO. The more you use LET GO for the little daily things, the more powerfully it can help you with those old things that might still be bothering you.

To LET GO of big things that bother you or hold you back, break it up into smaller parts and work letting go of one part at a time (however long it takes) and keep working it until all the parts have be LET GO.

## TELL US WHAT YOU JUST READ

You have just finished reading the LET GO Basics. The Basics consist of the weeks you study LET GO, the KEYWORDS, STATEMENT OF PURPOSE AND OWNERSHIP, OBJECTIVE, TOOL INTRO and HOW TO USE LET GO. Remember ALL GOGI Tools were written **by** prisoners **for** prisoners.

*In your own words, explain the GOGI Tool LET GO:* _____

_____

_____

_____

_____

_____

_____

_____

_____

_____

_____

_____

**DAILY SIGN-IN – GROUP CERTIFICATE COURSE**
If you want to receive credit, please fill out the information below:

The month is_____ The day of the month is _____ The year is_____ Signature _____
Meeting location_____ Start time _____ Number of people in my Group _____
MY GROUP STUDIES ACCORDING TO THE GOGI CALENDAR (circle one)     YES     NO

# LET GO Meeting

GOGI weeks begin on Monday. ONLY hold this meeting in the following weeks: (check the week you are studying the LET GO Tool.)

❑4th Week of February   ❑ 4th Week of May   ❑4th Week of August   ❑4th Week of November

## Call Your Meeting to Order

*To be read by a volunteer:*
We call this GOGI meeting to order. We are gathered here today as a GOGI community of like-minded individuals who CLAIM RESPONSIBILITY for our lives in our own unique ways. We include the GOGI TOOLS FOR POSITIVE DECISION-MAKING as a supplement to our existing or potential spiritual and social support systems. We believe that the GOGI Tools help us on our journey toward internal freedom regardless of any perceived differences among us. We realize the GOGI TOOLS FOR POSITIVE DECISION-MAKING are learned according to a calendar and they are simple tools that may enhance many other practices that promote our health and well-being. We acknowledge the GOGI Tools as positive decision-making tools to help us in our daily living.

## The GOGI Purpose

*To be read by a volunteer:*
The purpose of GOGI is to provide simple tools to anyone interested in making more positive decisions in their lives. We do this through sharing the GOGI Tools which are taught in many ways and formats including independent-study, small group study, as well as formal educational programming offering course credit provided by institutions or educational organizations. Our purpose is to offer these tools as a positive and prosocial culture, not as a program, even in instances where GOGI is studied in a program format. We study the GOGI Tools according to the GOGI Calendar so no one will ever be alone in their study of GOGI. The GOGI Tools are to be shared freely among all people and should not be withheld for any reason.

## Reading of Your Tools *(To be read by a volunteer:)*
## The GOGI TOOLS FOR POSITIVE DECISION-MAKING are:

| | |
|---|---|
| BOSS OF MY BRAIN | CLAIM RESPONSIBILITY |
| BELLY BREATHING | LET GO |
| FIVE SECOND LIGHTSWITCH | FOR–GIVE |
| POSITIVE THOUGHTS | WHAT IF |
| POSITIVE WORDS | REALITY CHECK |
| POSITIVE ACTIONS | ULTIMATE FREEDOM |

**DAILY SIGN-IN – GROUP CERTIFICATE COURSE**
**If you want to receive credit, please fill out the information below:**

The month is_____ The day of the month is _____ The year is_____ Signature _____
Meeting location_____ Start time _____ Number of people in my Group _____
MY GROUP STUDIES ACCORDING TO THE GOGI CALENDAR (circle one)   YES   NO

## This Week's Objective

*To be read by a volunteer:*
Your goal this week is to practice the power of putting problems in your HAND, then SQUASH them and TOSS them away. This tool, called LET GO, will permit you to HAND/SQUASH/TOSS anything that might stand in your way.

## Check in/Recap of Your Prior Week

A brief check in when group members share their progress with the tools.

## Your Group Discussion

Please have volunteers or preassigned group members read from any of the GOGI books. This can be anything from any of the GOGI books related to the tool of this week (according to the GOGI Calendar). You may wish to have multiple people read from different GOGI books.

## Your Group Questions and Activities

This is a perfect time to have an activity. Your group can discuss this tool and, if completing GOGI as a program for credit, now is a great time to review or have your group members complete any required written assignments.

## Close Your Meeting

*We invite you to join us for our next meeting to be held (date) where we will study the GOGI Tool: _____ (refer to Calendar). If we are unable to hold next week's meeting we will refer to the Calendar for the tool we will study at the next meeting. Course credit is earned by meeting twelve to fifteen times, even if tools are skipped or repeated.*

## GOGI Pledge

*To be read by a volunteer:*

*May our commitment (group repeat)*
*To the study of GOGI (group repeat)*
*Grant us the joy (group repeat)*
*Of giving and receiving (group repeat)*
*So that our inner freedom (group repeat)*
*May be of maximum service (group repeat)*
*To those we love (group repeat)*
*And infinite others (group repeat)*

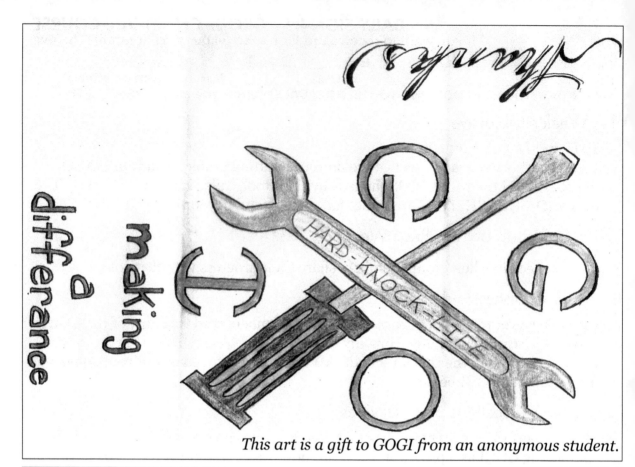

*This art is a gift to GOGI from an anonymous student.*

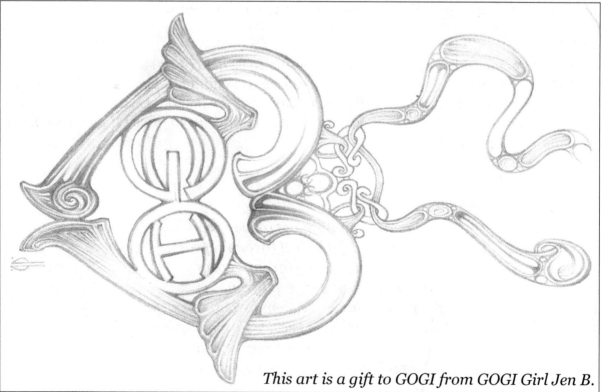

*This art is a gift to GOGI from GOGI Girl Jen B.*

## DAILY SIGN-IN – GROUP CERTIFICATE COURSE
### If you want to receive credit, please fill out the information below:

The month is_____ The day of the month is _____The year is_____ Signature _____
Meeting location_____ Start time _____ Number of people in my Group _____
MY GROUP STUDIES ACCORDING TO THE GOGI CALENDAR (circle one)     YES     NO

## Weekly Course Worksheet LET GO

*If you could choose one thing right now to HAND/SQUASH/TOSS, what would it be? Why?*_____

_____

_____

*Why is it so difficult for some people to LET GO of daily irritations, and why do you think it is important to LET GO of those daily irritations?*_____

_____

_____

_____

_____

*If you practice LET GO for the little stuff, how do you think it can help you LET GO of the big stuff that has been hard to move beyond?*_____

_____

_____

_____

*What situation in your life right now might be better if you use HAND/SQUASH/ TOSS?* _____

_____

*LET GO can have a powerful impact on your future life, why is it important to use LET GO to move forward?* _____

_____

*for self:* _____

*for family:* _____

*for friends:*_____

*for future:* _____

*for freedom:*_____

*This art is a gift to GOGI from Dana Harper, a free man 2018.*

# DAILY SIGN-IN – GROUP CERTIFICATE COURSE
## If you want to receive credit, please fill out the information below:

The month is_____ The day of the month is _____ The year is_____ Signature _____
Meeting location_____ Start time _____ Number of people in my Group _____
MY GROUP STUDIES ACCORDING TO THE GOGI CALENDAR (circle one)    YES    NO

## My GOGI Group Reflections

*In my GOGI Group this week I learned about the tool:* _____

_____

*This tool belongs to the section of tools called: The Tools of* _____

*I learned that this GOGI Tool has KEYWORDS. The KEYWORDS for this tool are:*

_____

_____

_____

*If I choose, I could apply this GOGI Tool to my daily life. Below is an example of how this tool might help me make better decisions:*_____

_____

_____

_____

*What I liked most about my GOGI Group this week was:* _____

_____

_____

*Meeting in a GOGI Group is helpful to my learning and growth because:* _____

_____

_____

*Here are some things I want to write down so that I do not forget them in the future. They are my thoughts and my observations about life and GOGI.* _____

_____

_____

_____

_____

# REMAIN ON THE GOGI CALENDAR

## Start the FOR—GIVE Meeting in 3 easy Steps

1. Check the **GOGI** Calendar before your meeting

2. Read the **GOGI** Tools Basics before your meeting

3. Enjoy your **GOGI** Meeting

# The GOGI FOR—GIVE Calendar
## For all GOGI meetings, remain on the GOGI calendar.

GOGI studies all tools according to the CALENDAR. GOGI weeks always start on Monday. Each month will start on Monday the 1st, 2nd, 3rd, 4th, 5th, 6th, or 7th. FOR—GIVE is studied by all GOGI students on the weeks circled below. Fifteen meetings makes one cycle of study. You might study one tool twice if a meeting was missed. That's okay!

### JANUARY
Week 1 BOSS OF MY BRAIN
Week 2 BELLY BREATHING
Week 3 FIVE SECOND LIGHTSWITCH
Week 4 POSITIVE THOUGHTS
Week 5 REVIEW ABOVE

### FEBRUARY
Week 1 POSITIVE WORDS
Week 2 POSITIVE ACTIONS
Week 3 CLAIM RESPONSIBILITY
Week 4 LET GO
Week 5 REVIEW ABOVE

### MARCH
Week 1 FOR–GIVE
Week 2 WHAT IF
Week 3 REALITY CHECK
Week 4 ULTIMATE FREEDOM
Week 5 REVIEW ABOVE

### APRIL
Week 1 BOSS OF MY BRAIN
Week 2 BELLY BREATHING
Week 3 FIVE SECOND LIGHTSWITCH
Week 4 POSITIVE THOUGHTS
Week 5 REVIEW ABOVE

### MAY
Week 1 POSITIVE WORDS
Week 2 POSITIVE ACTIONS
Week 3 CLAIM RESPONSIBILITY
Week 4 LET GO
Week 5 REVIEW ABOVE

### JUNE
Week 1 FOR–GIVE
Week 2 WHAT IF
Week 3 REALITY CHECK
Week 4 ULTIMATE FREEDOM
Week 5 REVIEW ABOVE

### JULY
Week 1 BOSS OF MY BRAIN
Week 2 BELLY BREATHING
Week 3 FIVE SECOND LIGHTSWITCH
Week 4 POSITIVE THOUGHTS
Week 5 REVIEW ABOVE

### AUGUST
Week 1 POSITIVE WORDS
Week 2 POSITIVE ACTIONS
Week 3 CLAIM RESPONSIBILITY
Week 4 LET GO
Week 5 REVIEW ABOVE

### SEPTEMBER
Week 1 FOR–GIVE
Week 2 WHAT IF
Week 3 REALITY CHECK
Week 4 ULTIMATE FREEDOM
Week 5 REVIEW ABOVE

### OCTOBER
Week 1 BOSS OF MY BRAIN
Week 2 BELLY BREATHING
Week 3 FIVE SECOND LIGHTSWITCH
Week 4 POSITIVE THOUGHTS
Week 5 REVIEW ABOVE

### NOVEMBER
Week 1 POSITIVE WORDS
Week 2 POSITIVE ACTIONS
Week 3 CLAIM RESPONSIBILITY
Week 4 LET GO
Week 5 REVIEW ABOVE

### DECEMBER
Week 1 FOR–GIVE
Week 2 WHAT IF
Week 3 REALITY CHECK
Week 4 ULTIMATE FREEDOM
Week 5 REVIEW ABOVE

**DAILY SIGN-IN – GROUP CERTIFICATE COURSE**
If you want to receive credit, please fill out the information below:

The month is_____ The day of the month is _____ The year is_____ Signature _____
Meeting location_____ Start time _____ Number of people in my Group _____
MY GROUP STUDIES ACCORDING TO THE GOGI CALENDAR (circle one)     YES     NO

# FOR–GIVE Basics

## Check the week you are holding this group study:

_____ 1st Week of March

_____ 1st Week of June

_____ 1st Week of September

_____ 1st Week of December

## KEYWORDS – FOR–GIVE

FOR ME TO GIVE, I NEED DISTANCE FROM HARM.

For me to give, I unhook from the past, and find my internal freedom.

## STATEMENT OF PURPOSE AND OWNERSHIP – FOR–GIVE

FOR me to GIVE back to others I make sure I am safe from harm. FOR me to GIVE, I make sure I am safe.

## OBJECTIVE – FOR–GIVE

This week you get to practice being the boss of how much past harm and past hurt you carry with you. You get to focus on being safe from more harm so that you can GIVE back to others and make your world a better place. FOR you to GIVE, you will learn to keep yourself safe.

## TOOL INTRO – FOR–GIVE

For you to be really happy, you will eventually discover that you need to give your time and energy to others to help them. This is how lasting happiness is created. But FOR you to GIVE, you need to get yourself safe from harm. FOR you to be a GIVING individual, you must be getting distance from addiction or abuse. You must be SAFE ENOUGH TO GIVE.

FOR–GIVE as a GOGI TOOL requires that you get yourself in a safe enough position so you can begin to give back to others.

## DAILY SIGN-IN – GROUP CERTIFICATE COURSE
### If you want to receive credit, please fill out the information below:

The month is_____ The day of the month is _____ The year is_____ Signature _____

Meeting location_____ Start time _____ Number of people in my Group _____

**MY GROUP STUDIES ACCORDING TO THE GOGI CALENDAR (circle one)    YES    NO**

## HOW TO USE – FOR–GIVE

As a tool, FOR–GIVE is about being safe enough for you to give back. This means if the harm is really close, you need to get to safety. If your addiction is the harm, you need to get to the safety offered by programs, churches, sober societies, and other support systems.

You need to be a sufficient distance from the person or circumstance that causes you harm. It is nearly impossible to use FOR–GIVE when the danger is right there in front of you. In fact, it is not wise to place an alcoholic in a bar, an addict next to a needle, or a thief next to unguarded jewels. FOR–GIVE is about protection. Make sure you and everyone around you is safe enough FOR you to GIVE back and FOR you to be the GIVING person you were meant to be.

## TELL US WHAT YOU JUST READ

You have just finished reading the FOR–GIVE Basics. The Basics consist of the weeks you study FOR–GIVE, the KEYWORDS, STATEMENT OF PURPOSE AND OWNERSHIP, OBJECTIVE, TOOL INTRO and HOW TO USE    FOR–GIVE. Remember ALL GOGI Tools were written **by** prisoners **for** prisoners.

*In your own words, explain the GOGI Tool FOR–GIVE:* _____

_____

_____

_____

_____

_____

_____

_____

_____

_____

**DAILY SIGN-IN – GROUP CERTIFICATE COURSE**
If you want to receive credit, please fill out the information below:

The month is_____ The day of the month is _____ The year is_____ Signature _____
Meeting location_____ Start time _____ Number of people in my Group _____
MY GROUP STUDIES ACCORDING TO THE GOGI CALENDAR (circle one)     YES     NO

# FOR–GIVE Meeting

GOGI weeks begin on Monday. ONLY hold this meeting in the following weeks: (check the week you are studying the FOR–GIVE Tool.)

❑ 1st Week of March     ❑ 1st Week of June     ❑ 1st Week of September     ❑ 1st Week of December

## Call Your Meeting to Order

*To be read by a volunteer:*

We call this GOGI meeting to order. We are gathered here today as a GOGI community of like-minded individuals who CLAIM RESPONSIBILITY for our lives in our own unique ways. We include the GOGI TOOLS FOR POSITIVE DECISION-MAKING as a supplement to our existing or potential spiritual and social support systems. We believe that the GOGI Tools help us on our journey toward internal freedom regardless of any perceived differences among us. We realize the GOGI TOOLS FOR POSITIVE DECISION-MAKING are learned according to a calendar and they are simple tools that may enhance many other practices that promote our health and well-being. We acknowledge the GOGI Tools as positive decision-making tools to help us in our daily living.

## The GOGI Purpose

*To be read by a volunteer:*

The purpose of GOGI is to provide simple tools to anyone interested in making more positive decisions in their lives. We do this through sharing the GOGI Tools which are taught in many ways and formats including independent-study, small group study, as well as formal educational programming offering course credit provided by institutions or educational organizations. Our purpose is to offer these tools as a positive and prosocial culture, not as a program, even in instances where GOGI is studied in a program format. We study the GOGI Tools according to the GOGI Calendar so no one will ever be alone in their study of GOGI. The GOGI Tools are to be shared freely among all people and should not be withheld for any reason.

## Reading of Your Tools *(To be read by a volunteer:)*

## The GOGI TOOLS FOR POSITIVE DECISION-MAKING are:

| | |
|---|---|
| BOSS OF MY BRAIN | CLAIM RESPONSIBILITY |
| BELLY BREATHING | LET GO |
| FIVE SECOND LIGHTSWITCH | FOR–GIVE |
| POSITIVE THOUGHTS | WHAT IF |
| POSITIVE WORDS | REALITY CHECK |
| POSITIVE ACTIONS | ULTIMATE FREEDOM |

The month is_____ The day of the month is _____The year is_____ Signature _____

Meeting location_____ Start time _____ Number of people in my Group _____

**MY GROUP STUDIES ACCORDING TO THE GOGI CALENDAR (circle one)    YES    NO**

## This Week's Objective

*To be read by a volunteer:*

This week you get to practice being the boss of how much past harm and past hurt you carry with you. You get to focus on being safe from more harm so that you can GIVE back to others and make our world a better place. FOR you to GIVE, you will learn to keep yourself safe.

## Check in/Recap of Your Prior Week

A brief check in when group members share their progress with the tools.

## Your Group Discussion

Please have volunteers or preassigned group members read from any of the GOGI books. This can be anything from any of the GOGI books related to the tool of this week (according to the GOGI Calendar). You may wish to have multiple people read from different GOGI books.

## Your Group Questions and Activities

This is a perfect time to have an activity. Your group can discuss this tool and, if completing GOGI as a program for credit, now is a great time to review or have your group members complete any required written assignments.

## Close Your Meeting

*We invite you to join us for our next meeting to be held (date) where we will study the GOGI Tool: _____ (refer to Calendar). If we are unable to hold next week's meeting we will refer to the Calendar for the tool we will study at the next meeting. Course credit is earned by meeting twelve to fifteen times, even if tools are skipped or repeated.*

## GOGI Pledge

*To be read by a volunteer:*

> *May our commitment (group repeat)*
> *To the study of GOGI (group repeat)*
> *Grant us the joy (group repeat)*
> *Of giving and receiving (group repeat)*
> *So that our inner freedom (group repeat)*
> *May be of maximum service (group repeat)*
> *To those we love (group repeat)*
> *And infinite others (group repeat)*

## DAILY SIGN-IN – GROUP CERTIFICATE COURSE
**If you want to receive credit, please fill out the information below:**

The month is_____ The day of the month is _____ The year is_____ Signature _____
Meeting location_____ Start time _____ Number of people in my Group _____
**MY GROUP STUDIES ACCORDING TO THE GOGI CALENDAR (circle one)     YES     NO**

## Weekly Course Worksheet FOR–GIVE

*What does 'You must be SAFE ENOUGH TO GIVE' mean to you?* _____

_____

_____

*What are some things you can stay away from so you can give back to others?* _____

_____

_____

*FOR–GIVE, as a tool, is different from forgive as an action. How would you explain FOR–GIVE to a friend? The tool FOR—GIVE IS:* _____

_____

_____

_____

*The action of forgiveness is:* _____

_____

_____

_____

*How can you distance yourself from harm so you can use the tool FOR–GIVE? I can...*_____

_____

_____

_____

*How would you give back to others using the tool FOR–GIVE?* _____

_____

*When I am safe from harm, I can give to others by...* _____

_____

| **Before I was the BOSS OF MY BRAIN** | **Now that I am BOSS OF MY BRAIN** |
|---|---|
| Im A good Bro | Im A great DAD |
| Im A good Bike Mechanic | Im A great Bike Mecha |
| Im A good Musician | Im A great musician |
| Im A good fighter | I Dont need to fight |
| Im Stubborn | Im flexible |
| Im Implosive | I express Myself Correctly |
| Im Selfish | Im thoughtful + Generous |
| Im Tired | Im energetic |
| Im On Drugs | Im CleAn! 😊 |
| My family Didnt come 1st | My family is Everything |
| Im Impulsive | I use the SMArt part of my |
| Im undecided | I know which PAth Im goin |
| Im Overwelmed | I cAn handle things one At A time As they |
| Im without Direction | Im StrAight Ahead! |
| My family Misses me | I miss my family |

*This art is a gift to GOGI from an anonymous student.*

# DAILY SIGN-IN – GROUP CERTIFICATE COURSE
### If you want to receive credit, please fill out the information below:

The month is_____ The day of the month is _____The year is_____ Signature _____
Meeting location_____ Start time _____ Number of people in my Group _____
**MY GROUP STUDIES ACCORDING TO THE GOGI CALENDAR (circle one)     YES      NO**

## My GOGI Group Reflections

*In my GOGI Group this week I learned about the tool:* _____

_____

*This tool belongs to the section of tools called: The Tools of* _____

*I learned that this GOGI Tool has KEYWORDS. The KEYWORDS for this tool are:*

_____

_____

_____

*If I choose, I could apply this GOGI Tool to my daily life. Below is an example of how this tool might help me make better decisions:*_____

_____

_____

_____

*What I liked most about my GOGI Group this week was:* _____

_____

_____

*Meeting in a GOGI Group is helpful to my learning and growth because:* _____

_____

_____

*Here are some things I want to write down so that I do not forget them in the future. They are my thoughts and my observations about life and GOGI.* _____

_____

_____

_____

_____

# REMAIN ON THE
# GOGI
# CALENDAR

## Start the
## WHAT IF

## Meeting in 3 easy Steps

1. **Check the GOGI Calendar before your meeting**

2. **Read the GOGI Tools Basics before your meeting**

3. **Enjoy your GOGI Meeting**

# The GOGI WHAT IF Calendar
## For all GOGI meetings, remain on the GOGI calendar.

GOGI studies all tools according to the CALENDAR. GOGI weeks always start on Monday. Each month will start on Monday the 1st, 2nd, 3rd, 4th, 5th, 6th, or 7th. WHAT IF is studied by all GOGI students on the weeks circled below. Fifteen meetings makes one cycle of study. You might study one tool twice if a meeting was missed. That's okay!

### JANUARY
Week 1 BOSS OF MY BRAIN
Week 2 BELLY BREATHING
Week 3 FIVE SECOND LIGHTSWITCH
Week 4 POSITIVE THOUGHTS
Week 5 REVIEW ABOVE

### FEBRUARY
Week 1 POSITIVE WORDS
Week 2 POSITIVE ACTIONS
Week 3 CLAIM RESPONSIBILITY
Week 4 LET GO
Week 5 REVIEW ABOVE

### MARCH
Week 1 FOR–GIVE
Week 2 WHAT IF
Week 3 REALITY CHECK
Week 4 ULTIMATE FREEDOM
Week 5 REVIEW ABOVE

### APRIL
Week 1 BOSS OF MY BRAIN
Week 2 BELLY BREATHING
Week 3 FIVE SECOND LIGHTSWITCH
Week 4 POSITIVE THOUGHTS
Week 5 REVIEW ABOVE

### MAY
Week 1 POSITIVE WORDS
Week 2 POSITIVE ACTIONS
Week 3 CLAIM RESPONSIBILITY
Week 4 LET GO
Week 5 REVIEW ABOVE

### JUNE
Week 1 FOR–GIVE
Week 2 WHAT IF
Week 3 REALITY CHECK
Week 4 ULTIMATE FREEDOM
Week 5 REVIEW ABOVE

### JULY
Week 1 BOSS OF MY BRAIN
Week 2 BELLY BREATHING
Week 3 FIVE SECOND LIGHTSWITCH
Week 4 POSITIVE THOUGHTS
Week 5 REVIEW ABOVE

### AUGUST
Week 1 POSITIVE WORDS
Week 2 POSITIVE ACTIONS
Week 3 CLAIM RESPONSIBILITY
Week 4 LET GO
Week 5 REVIEW ABOVE

### SEPTEMBER
Week 1 FOR–GIVE
Week 2 WHAT IF
Week 3 REALITY CHECK
Week 4 ULTIMATE FREEDOM
Week 5 REVIEW ABOVE

### OCTOBER
Week 1 BOSS OF MY BRAIN
Week 2 BELLY BREATHING
Week 3 FIVE SECOND LIGHTSWITCH
Week 4 POSITIVE THOUGHTS
Week 5 REVIEW ABOVE

### NOVEMBER
Week 1 POSITIVE WORDS
Week 2 POSITIVE ACTIONS
Week 3 CLAIM RESPONSIBILITY
Week 4 LET GO
Week 5 REVIEW ABOVE

### DECEMBER
Week 1 FOR–GIVE
Week 2 WHAT IF
Week 3 REALITY CHECK
Week 4 ULTIMATE FREEDOM
Week 5 REVIEW ABOVE

# WHAT IF Basics

## Check the week you are holding this group study:

____    2nd Week of March

____    2nd Week of June

____    2nd Week of September

____    2nd Week of December

## KEYWORDS – WHAT IF

WHAT IF I AM NOT MY PAST?
No to the past = Yes to the future.

## STATEMENT OF PURPOSE AND OWNERSHIP – WHAT IF

WHAT IF permits me to see possibilities I might not otherwise realize. Today, I ask myself, WHAT IF I am not my past? WHAT IF I reached my goal? WHAT IF I actually improved my life today, tomorrow, and the next day?

## OBJECTIVE – WHAT IF

Your goal this week is to be the boss of your future. You do this by asking the WHAT IF question, because when you look at the possible outcome for the future you will make better decisions in the present. WHAT IF is the tool you can use to build your positive future.

## TOOL INTRO – WHAT IF

The tool WHAT IF is really cool because it gives you a glimpse into what might be possible. You can use WHAT IF for the negative to avoid negative outcomes. You can also use WHAT IF for the positive, to see new positive possibilities. WHAT IF is your ability to look into the future and see the likely outcome of any action you take. With this ability, you can set goals for yourself and clearly see the benefit of working toward a positive outcome. WHAT IF you are not your past? This critical question frees you to become a benefit to society because of your past! WHAT IF you are needed as the solution?

## DAILY SIGN-IN – GROUP CERTIFICATE COURSE
### If you want to receive credit, please fill out the information below:

The month is_____ The day of the month is _____The year is_____ Signature _____

Meeting location_____ Start time _____ Number of people in my Group _____

**MY GROUP STUDIES ACCORDING TO THE GOGI CALENDAR (circle one)   YES   NO**

## HOW TO USE – WHAT IF

You can use the GOGI Tool WHAT IF for everything you do during the day. WHAT IF you wake up early? WHAT IF you don't? WHAT IF you go to that meeting? WHAT IF you don't? WHAT IF places you in charge, because you are choosing every minute of the day what you want to endorse in your life. You are checking out the possible outcomes with the WHAT IF tool and you are clearly stating the direction of your life from now onward. WHAT IF can permit you a glimpse into the future. You can say "WHAT IF I don't go to a meeting and I start thinking about drinking?" You can also say, "WHAT IF I do go to a meeting and I am able to sit with other people who are on a positive path?" WHAT IF gives you a snapshot of what is likely to happen with your decision.

## TELL US WHAT YOU JUST READ

You have just finished reading the WHAT IF Basics. The Basics consist of the weeks you study WHAT IF, the KEYWORDS, STATEMENT OF PURPOSE AND OWNERSHIP, OBJECTIVE, TOOL INTRO and HOW TO USE WHAT IF. Remember ALL GOGI Tools were written **by** prisoners **for** prisoners.

*In your own words, explain the GOGI Tool WHAT IF:* _____

_____

_____

_____

_____

_____

_____

_____

_____

_____

_____

**DAILY SIGN-IN – GROUP CERTIFICATE COURSE**
If you want to receive credit, please fill out the information below:

The month is_____ The day of the month is _____ The year is_____ Signature _____
Meeting location_____ Start time _____ Number of people in my Group _____
MY GROUP STUDIES ACCORDING TO THE GOGI CALENDAR (circle one)    YES    NO

# WHAT IF Meeting

GOGI weeks begin on Monday. ONLY hold this meeting in the following weeks: (check the week you are studying the WHAT IF Tool.)

❏ 2nd Week of March    ❏ 2nd Week of June    ❏ 2nd Week of September    ❏ 2nd Week of December

## Call Your Meeting to Order

*To be read by a volunteer:*
We call this GOGI meeting to order. We are gathered here today as a GOGI community of like-minded individuals who CLAIM RESPONSIBILITY for our lives in our own unique ways. We include the GOGI TOOLS FOR POSITIVE DECISION-MAKING as a supplement to our existing or potential spiritual and social support systems. We believe that the GOGI Tools help us on our journey toward internal freedom regardless of any perceived differences among us. We realize the GOGI TOOLS FOR POSITIVE DECISION-MAKING are learned according to a calendar and they are simple tools that may enhance many other practices that promote our health and well-being. We acknowledge the GOGI Tools as positive decision-making tools to help us in our daily living.

## The GOGI Purpose

*To be read by a volunteer:*
The purpose of GOGI is to provide simple tools to anyone interested in making more positive decisions in their lives. We do this through sharing the GOGI Tools which are taught in many ways and formats including independent-study, small group study, as well as formal educational programming offering course credit provided by institutions or educational organizations. Our purpose is to offer these tools as a positive and prosocial culture, not as a program, even in instances where GOGI is studied in a program format. We study the GOGI Tools according to the GOGI Calendar so no one will ever be alone in their study of GOGI. The GOGI Tools are to be shared freely among all people and should not be withheld for any reason.

## Reading of Your Tools *(To be read by a volunteer:)*

## The GOGI TOOLS FOR POSITIVE DECISION-MAKING are:

| | |
|---|---|
| BOSS OF MY BRAIN | CLAIM RESPONSIBILITY |
| BELLY BREATHING | LET GO |
| FIVE SECOND LIGHTSWITCH | FOR–GIVE |
| POSITIVE THOUGHTS | WHAT IF |
| POSITIVE WORDS | REALITY CHECK |
| POSITIVE ACTIONS | ULTIMATE FREEDOM |

## DAILY SIGN-IN – GROUP CERTIFICATE COURSE
### If you want to receive credit, please fill out the information below:

The month is_____ The day of the month is _____ The year is_____ Signature _____

Meeting location_____ Start time _____ Number of people in my Group _____

**MY GROUP STUDIES ACCORDING TO THE GOGI CALENDAR (circle one)     YES     NO**

## This Week's Objective

*To be read by a volunteer:*

Your goal this week is to be the boss of your future. You do this by asking the WHAT IF question, because when you look at the possible outcomes for the future you will make better decisions in the present. WHAT IF is the tool you can use to build your positive future.

## Check in/Recap of Your Prior Week

A brief check in when group members share their progress with the tools.

## Your Group Discussion

Please have volunteers or preassigned group members read from any of the GOGI books. This can be anything from any of the GOGI books related to the tool of this week (according to the GOGI Calendar). You may wish to have multiple people read from different GOGI books.

## Your Group Questions and Activities

This is a perfect time to have an activity. Your group can discuss this tool and, if completing GOGI as a program for credit, now is a great time to review or have your group members complete any required written assignments.

## Close Your Meeting

*We invite you to join us for our next meeting to be held (date) where we will study the GOGI Tool: _____ (refer to Calendar). If we are unable to hold next week's meeting we will refer to the Calendar for the tool we will study at the next meeting. Course credit is earned by meeting twelve to fifteen times, even if tools are skipped or repeated.*

## GOGI Pledge

*To be read by a volunteer:*

*May our commitment (group repeat)*
*To the study of GOGI (group repeat)*
*Grant us the joy (group repeat)*
*Of giving and receiving (group repeat)*
*So that our inner freedom (group repeat)*
*May be of maximum service (group repeat)*
*To those we love (group repeat)*
*And infinite others (group repeat)*

## DAILY SIGN-IN – GROUP CERTIFICATE COURSE
### If you want to receive credit, please fill out the information below:

The month is_____ The day of the month is _____The year is_____ Signature _____
Meeting location_____ Start time _____ Number of people in my Group _____
MY GROUP STUDIES ACCORDING TO THE GOGI CALENDAR (circle one)    YES    NO

## Weekly Course Worksheet WHAT IF?

Most GOGI students say that WHAT IF allows them to say "yes" to the future. What do you see in your future if you are not limited by your past? _____

_____

In my future I see... _____

_____

Some GOGI students say, "I could have done..." or "I should have done..." How does WHAT IF change what they say? Because the GOGI tool WHAT IF... _____

_____

_____

_____

WHAT IF gives you the ability to say "yes" to the future. What will you say "yes" to in your future? What in your past will you say "no more" to? _____

I say "yes" to: _____

_____

_____

I say "no more" to: _____

_____

_____

The tool WHAT IF says you are not your past. Why is that important to so many GOGI students? _____

_____

_____

How is not being limited by your past important to you? _____

_____

_____

GOD

Toolbelt

Ready, Set, Go

Drawn By
Frank
C.
Mercier III
9-19-13

1.) Boss of my Brain = had to rewire my brain for positiveness.

2.) Belly Breathing = had to breathe properly so I can make positive choices.

3.) Five Second Light Switch = had to flip the switch on my smart port finally.

4.) Positive Thoughts = had to be positive in thoughtfulness..

5.) Positive Words = had to have positive words with my internal change.

6.) Positive Actions = had to respond positively physically, mentally to lifes challenges.

7.) Claim Responsibility = had to check myself first in my brain for healthy outcomes.

8.) Let Go = had to let go of past life disappointments.

9.) Forgive = had to disassociate myself from all negative Elements of people, places, things.

10.) What If = had to map out my positive future.

11.) Reality Check = had keep inching forward when I'm not perfect.

12.) Ultimate Freedom = had to have inner peace so I can be of kind service

# DAILY SIGN-IN – GROUP CERTIFICATE COURSE

**If you want to receive credit, please fill out the information below:**

The month is_____ The day of the month is _____ The year is_____ Signature _____

Meeting location_____ Start time _____ Number of people in my Group _____

**MY GROUP STUDIES ACCORDING TO THE GOGI CALENDAR (circle one)     YES     NO**

## My GOGI Group Reflections

In my GOGI Group this week I learned about the tool: _____

_____

This tool belongs to the section of tools called: The Tools of _____

I learned that this GOGI Tool has KEYWORDS. The KEYWORDS for this tool are:

_____

_____

_____

If I choose, I could apply this GOGI Tool to my daily life. Below is an example of how this tool might help me make better decisions:_____

_____

_____

_____

What I liked most about my GOGI Group this week was: _____

_____

_____

Meeting in a GOGI Group is helpful to my learning and growth because: _____

_____

_____

Here are some things I want to write down so that I do not forget them in the future. They are my thoughts and my observations about life and GOGI. _____

_____

_____

_____

_____

# REMAIN ON THE
# GOGI
# CALENDAR

# Start the
# REALITY CHECK
## Meeting in 3 easy Steps

1. **Check the GOGI Calendar before your meeting**

2. **Read the GOGI Tools Basics before your meeting**

3. **Enjoy your GOGI Meeting**

# The GOGI REALITY CHECK Calendar
## For all GOGI meetings, remain on the GOGI calendar.

GOGI studies all tools according to the CALENDAR. GOGI weeks always start on Monday. Each month will start on Monday the 1st, 2nd, 3rd, 4th, 5th, 6th, or 7th. WHAT IF is studied by all GOGI students on the weeks circled below. Fifteen meetings makes one cycle of study. You might study one tool twice if a meeting was missed. That's okay!

### JANUARY
Week 1 BOSS OF MY BRAIN
Week 2 BELLY BREATHING
Week 3 FIVE SECOND LIGHTSWITCH
Week 4 POSITIVE THOUGHTS
Week 5 REVIEW ABOVE

### FEBRUARY
Week 1 POSITIVE WORDS
Week 2 POSITIVE ACTIONS
Week 3 CLAIM RESPONSIBILITY
Week 4 LET GO
Week 5 REVIEW ABOVE

### MARCH
Week 1 FOR–GIVE
Week 2 WHAT IF
Week 3 REALITY CHECK
Week 4 ULTIMATE FREEDOM
Week 5 REVIEW ABOVE

### APRIL
Week 1 BOSS OF MY BRAIN
Week 2 BELLY BREATHING
Week 3 FIVE SECOND LIGHTSWITCH
Week 4 POSITIVE THOUGHTS
Week 5 REVIEW ABOVE

### MAY
Week 1 POSITIVE WORDS
Week 2 POSITIVE ACTIONS
Week 3 CLAIM RESPONSIBILITY
Week 4 LET GO
Week 5 REVIEW ABOVE

### JUNE
Week 1 FOR–GIVE
Week 2 WHAT IF
Week 3 REALITY CHECK
Week 4 ULTIMATE FREEDOM
Week 5 REVIEW ABOVE

### JULY
Week 1 BOSS OF MY BRAIN
Week 2 BELLY BREATHING
Week 3 FIVE SECOND LIGHTSWITCH
Week 4 POSITIVE THOUGHTS
Week 5 REVIEW ABOVE

### AUGUST
Week 1 POSITIVE WORDS
Week 2 POSITIVE ACTIONS
Week 3 CLAIM RESPONSIBILITY
Week 4 LET GO
Week 5 REVIEW ABOVE

### SEPTEMBER
Week 1 FOR–GIVE
Week 2 WHAT IF
Week 3 REALITY CHECK
Week 4 ULTIMATE FREEDOM
Week 5 REVIEW ABOVE

### OCTOBER
Week 1 BOSS OF MY BRAIN
Week 2 BELLY BREATHING
Week 3 FIVE SECOND LIGHTSWITCH
Week 4 POSITIVE THOUGHTS
Week 5 REVIEW ABOVE

### NOVEMBER
Week 1 POSITIVE WORDS
Week 2 POSITIVE ACTIONS
Week 3 CLAIM RESPONSIBILITY
Week 4 LET GO
Week 5 REVIEW ABOVE

### DECEMBER
Week 1 FOR–GIVE
Week 2 WHAT IF
Week 3 REALITY CHECK
Week 4 ULTIMATE FREEDOM
Week 5 REVIEW ABOVE

**DAILY SIGN-IN – GROUP CERTIFICATE COURSE**
If you want to receive credit, please fill out the information below:

The month is_____ The day of the month is _____The year is_____ Signature _____
Meeting location_____ Start time _____ Number of people in my Group _____
MY GROUP STUDIES ACCORDING TO THE GOGI CALENDAR (circle one)    YES    NO

# REALITY CHECK Basics

## Check the week you are holding this group study:

_____ 3rd Week of March

_____ 3rd Week of June

_____ 3rd Week of September

_____ 3rd Week of December

## KEYWORDS – REALITY CHECK

TEN AND TWO RULE – Ten steps forward and two steps back is still eight steps ahead. Focus on your wins, not your losses.

## STATEMENT OF PURPOSE AND OWNERSHIP – REALITY CHECK

I know I am going to make mistakes along the way, but REALITY CHECK lets me quickly correct my mistakes. Today, I agree to get right back on track with REALITY CHECK when I do something that is not perfect.

## OBJECTIVE – REALITY CHECK

Your goal this week is to realize that you are human and you will make mistakes, but that does not mean you are not successful. This week's tool, REALITY CHECK, permits you to be the boss and recover from bad decisions quickly.

## TOOL INTRO – REALITY CHECK

The fact is you are human. You are not perfect. You will make bad decisions, GOGI realizes and accepts that humans make poor decisions. However, GOGI realizes that humans do not need to remain in bad decision-making mode.

If you take ten steps forward and two steps backward, you are still eight steps ahead. With GOGI, REALITY CHECK states that we focus on the GOOD and the PROGRESS rather than the poor decision.

For as long as you are human, you may make bad decisions, but your ability to get back on track quickly is your REALITY CHECK.

## HOW TO USE – REALITY CHECK

You can use REALITY CHECK with others and with yourself. Instead of focusing on the bad decisions, you focus on the improvements.

Focus on the positive. This will make it easier to overcome the disappointment that naturally comes when we make bad decisions.

Just say to yourself, "Ten steps forward and two steps back is still eight steps ahead." This will remind you that you are moving forward and give you your REALITY CHECK.

## TELL US WHAT YOU JUST READ

You have just finished reading the REALITY CHECK Basics. The Basics consist of the weeks you study REALITY CHECK, the KEYWORDS, STATEMENT OF PURPOSE AND OWNERSHIP, OBJECTIVE, TOOL INTRO and HOW TO USE REALITY CHECK. Remember ALL GOGI Tools were written *by* prisoners *for* prisoners.

*In your own words, explain the GOGI Tool REALITY CHECK:*_____

_____

_____

_____

_____

_____

_____

_____

_____

_____

## DAILY SIGN-IN – GROUP CERTIFICATE COURSE

If you want to receive credit, please fill out the information below:

The month is_____ The day of the month is _____ The year is_____ Signature _____

Meeting location_____ Start time _____ Number of people in my Group _____

MY GROUP STUDIES ACCORDING TO THE GOGI CALENDAR (circle one)     YES     NO

# REALITY CHECK Meeting

GOGI weeks begin on Monday. ONLY hold this meeting in the following weeks: (check the week you are studying the REALITY CHECK Tool.)

❑3rd Week of March     ❑3rd Week of June     ❑ 3rd Week of September     ❑ 3rd Week of December

## Call Your Meeting to Order

*To be read by a volunteer:*

We call this GOGI meeting to order. We are gathered here today as a GOGI community of like-minded individuals who CLAIM RESPONSIBILITY for our lives in our own unique ways. We include the GOGI TOOLS FOR POSITIVE DECISION-MAKING as a supplement to our existing or potential spiritual and social support systems. We believe that the GOGI Tools help us on our journey toward internal freedom regardless of any perceived differences among us. We realize the GOGI TOOLS FOR POSITIVE DECISION-MAKING are learned according to a calendar and they are simple tools that may enhance many other practices that promote our health and well-being. We acknowledge the GOGI Tools as positive decision-making tools to help us in our daily living.

## The GOGI Purpose

*To be read by a volunteer:*

The purpose of GOGI is to provide simple tools to anyone interested in making more positive decisions in their lives. We do this through sharing the GOGI Tools which are taught in many ways and formats including independent-study, small group study, as well as formal educational programming offering course credit provided by institutions or educational organizations. Our purpose is to offer these tools as a positive and prosocial culture, not as a program, even in instances where GOGI is studied in a program format. We study the GOGI Tools according to the GOGI Calendar so no one will ever be alone in their study of GOGI. The GOGI Tools are to be shared freely among all people and should not be withheld for any reason.

## Reading of Your Tools *(To be read by a volunteer:)*

# The GOGI TOOLS FOR POSITIVE DECISION-MAKING are:

| | |
|---|---|
| BOSS OF MY BRAIN | CLAIM RESPONSIBILITY |
| BELLY BREATHING | LET GO |
| FIVE SECOND LIGHTSWITCH | FOR–GIVE |
| POSITIVE THOUGHTS | WHAT IF |
| POSITIVE WORDS | REALITY CHECK |
| POSITIVE ACTIONS | ULTIMATE FREEDOM |

# DAILY SIGN-IN – GROUP CERTIFICATE COURSE
**If you want to receive credit, please fill out the information below:**

The month is_____ The day of the month is _____The year is_____ Signature _____
Meeting location_____ Start time _____ Number of people in my Group _____
**MY GROUP STUDIES ACCORDING TO THE GOGI CALENDAR (circle one)   YES   NO**

## This Week's Objective

*To be read by a volunteer:*
Your goal this week is to realize that you are human and you will make mistakes, but that does not mean you are not successful. This week's tool, REALITY CHECK, permits you to be the boss and recover from your bad decisions quickly.

## Check in/Recap of Your Prior Week

A brief check in when group members share their progress with the tools.

## Your Group Discussion

Please have volunteers or preassigned group members read from any of the GOGI books. This can be anything from any of the GOGI books related to the tool of this week (according to the GOGI Calendar). You may wish to have multiple people read from different GOGI books.

## Your Group Questions and Activities

This is a perfect time to have an activity. Your group can discuss this tool and, if completing GOGI as a program for credit, now is a great time to review or have your group members complete any required written assignments.

## Close Your Meeting

*We invite you to join us for our next meeting to be held (date) where we will study the GOGI Tool: _____ (refer to Calendar). If we are unable to hold next week's meeting we will refer to the Calendar for the tool we will study at the next meeting. Course credit is earned by meeting twelve to fifteen times, even if tools are skipped or repeated.*

## GOGI Pledge

*To be read by a volunteer:*

*May our commitment (group repeat)*
*To the study of GOGI (group repeat)*
*Grant us the joy (group repeat)*
*Of giving and receiving (group repeat)*
*So that our inner freedom (group repeat)*
*May be of maximum service (group repeat)*
*To those we love (group repeat)*
*And infinite others (group repeat)*

ART BY HARO.

*Art is a gift to GOGI by Haro.*

## DAILY SIGN-IN – GROUP CERTIFICATE COURSE
**If you want to receive credit, please fill out the information below:**

The month is_____ The day of the month is _____ The year is_____ Signature _____

Meeting location_____ Start time _____ Number of people in my Group _____

MY GROUP STUDIES ACCORDING TO THE GOGI CALENDAR (circle one)    YES    NO

## Weekly Course Worksheet REALITY CHECK

*The TEN AND TWO RULE is a very important part of the GOGI Tool REALITY CHECK. Most GOGI students don't remember their progress without using this tool. Why is it so difficult to remember the good things?*_____

_____

*Why do many people give up when the back track and weaken?* _____

_____

_____

*When you do make a mistake—and all humans make mistakes—how can you use REALITY CHECK to get out of your bad decision-making mode?*_____

_____

*How helpful could this tool be for friends and family?* _____

_____

_____

Using the REALITY CHECK tool allows you to focus on your improvements and good decisions, rather than just the bad decisions or actions.

*How does REALITY CHECK interact with POSITIVE THOUGHTS, POSITIVE WORDS, and POSITIVE ACTIONS?*_____

_____

*How does REALITY CHECK work with BOSS OF MY BRAIN?*_____

_____

*How does REALITY CHECK work with BELLY BREATHING?*_____

_____

*How does REALITY CHECK work with FIVE SECOND LIGHTSWITCH?* _____

_____

_____

This art is a gift to GOGI from Justin Allee.

## DAILY SIGN-IN – GROUP CERTIFICATE COURSE
### If you want to receive credit, please fill out the information below:

The month is_____ The day of the month is _____ The year is_____ Signature _____

Meeting location_____ Start time _____ Number of people in my Group _____

**MY GROUP STUDIES ACCORDING TO THE GOGI CALENDAR (circle one)    YES    NO**

## My GOGI Group Reflections

*In my GOGI Group this week I learned about the tool:* _____

_____

*This tool belongs to the section of tools called: The Tools of* _____

*I learned that this GOGI Tool has KEYWORDS. The KEYWORDS for this tool are:*

_____

_____

_____

*If I choose, I could apply this GOGI Tool to my daily life. Below is an example of how this tool might help me make better decisions:*_____

_____

_____

_____

*What I liked most about my GOGI Group this week was:* _____

_____

_____

*Meeting in a GOGI Group is helpful to my learning and growth because:* _____

_____

_____

*Here are some things I want to write down so that I do not forget them in the future. They are my thoughts and my observations about life and GOGI.* _____

_____

_____

_____

_____

# REMAIN ON THE GOGI CALENDAR

## Start the ULTIMATE FREEDOM Meeting in 3 easy Steps

1. Check the **GOGI Calendar** before your meeting

2. Read the **GOGI Tools Basics** before your meeting

3. Enjoy your **GOGI Meeting**

# The GOGI ULTIMATE FREEDOM Calendar
## For all GOGI meetings, remain on the GOGI calendar.

GOGI studies all tools according to the CALENDAR. GOGI weeks always start on Monday. Each month will start on Monday the 1st, 2nd, 3rd, 4th, 5th, 6th, or 7th. ULTIMATE FREEDOM is studied by all GOGI students on the weeks circled below. Fifteen meetings makes one cycle of study. You might study one tool twice if a meeting was missed. That's okay!

### JANUARY
Week 1 BOSS OF MY BRAIN
Week 2 BELLY BREATHING
Week 3 FIVE SECOND LIGHTSWITCH
Week 4 POSITIVE THOUGHTS
Week 5 REVIEW ABOVE

### FEBRUARY
Week 1 POSITIVE WORDS
Week 2 POSITIVE ACTIONS
Week 3 CLAIM RESPONSIBILITY
Week 4 LET GO
Week 5 REVIEW ABOVE

### MARCH
Week 1 FOR-GIVE
Week 2 WHAT IF
Week 3 REALITY CHECK
Week 4 ULTIMATE FREEDOM
Week 5 REVIEW ABOVE

### APRIL
Week 1 BOSS OF MY BRAIN
Week 2 BELLY BREATHING
Week 3 FIVE SECOND LIGHTSWITCH
Week 4 POSITIVE THOUGHTS
Week 5 REVIEW ABOVE

### MAY
Week 1 POSITIVE WORDS
Week 2 POSITIVE ACTIONS
Week 3 CLAIM RESPONSIBILITY
Week 4 LET GO
Week 5 REVIEW ABOVE

### JUNE
Week 1 FOR-GIVE
Week 2 WHAT IF
Week 3 REALITY CHECK
Week 4 ULTIMATE FREEDOM
Week 5 REVIEW ABOVE

### JULY
Week 1 BOSS OF MY BRAIN
Week 2 BELLY BREATHING
Week 3 FIVE SECOND LIGHTSWITCH
Week 4 POSITIVE THOUGHTS
Week 5 REVIEW ABOVE

### AUGUST
Week 1 POSITIVE WORDS
Week 2 POSITIVE ACTIONS
Week 3 CLAIM RESPONSIBILITY
Week 4 LET GO
Week 5 REVIEW ABOVE

### SEPTEMBER
Week 1 FOR-GIVE
Week 2 WHAT IF
Week 3 REALITY CHECK
Week 4 ULTIMATE FREEDOM
Week 5 REVIEW ABOVE

### OCTOBER
Week 1 BOSS OF MY BRAIN
Week 2 BELLY BREATHING
Week 3 FIVE SECOND LIGHTSWITCH
Week 4 POSITIVE THOUGHTS
Week 5 REVIEW ABOVE

### NOVEMBER
Week 1 POSITIVE WORDS
Week 2 POSITIVE ACTIONS
Week 3 CLAIM RESPONSIBILITY
Week 4 LET GO
Week 5 REVIEW ABOVE

### DECEMBER
Week 1 FOR-GIVE
Week 2 WHAT IF
Week 3 REALITY CHECK
Week 4 ULTIMATE FREEDOM
Week 5 REVIEW ABOVE

**DAILY SIGN-IN – GROUP CERTIFICATE COURSE**
If you want to receive credit, please fill out the information below:

The month is_____ The day of the month is _____ The year is_____ Signature _____
Meeting location_____ Start time _____ Number of people in my Group _____
MY GROUP STUDIES ACCORDING TO THE GOGI CALENDAR (circle one)    YES    NO

# ULTIMATE FREEDOM Basics

## Check the week you are holding this group study:

_____ 4th Week of March

_____ 4th Week of June

_____ 4th Week of September

_____ 4th Week of December

## KEYWORDS – ULTIMATE FREEDOM

BEING FREE IS UP TO ME.

Living a life of service gives me ULTIMATE FREEDOM.

## STATEMENT OF PURPOSE AND OWNERSHIP – ULTIMATE FREEDOM

I create ULTIMATE FREEDOM for myself when I live THE GOGI WAY. Through my service, I have ULTIMATE FREEDOM.

## OBJECTIVE – ULTIMATE FREEDOM

Your goal this week is to practice creating freedom in your life by doing good things, even when no one is looking. ULTIMATE FREEDOM is this week's tool, you can be the boss of your level of freedom when you practice ULTIMATE FREEDOM each day.

## TOOL INTRO – ULTIMATE FREEDOM

ULTIMATE FREEDOM is a feeling inside you that no one and no situation can take away. ULTIMATE FREEDOM is also something you are in charge of creating for yourself. ULTIMATE FREEDOM is available for everyone, not just a few people who have something you do not.

ULTIMATE FREEDOM is the freedom that comes when you decide to live your life in service of others. When you choose to live your life for something more than your own desires and needs, you begin to feel the little sparks of ULTIMATE FREEDOM.

## DAILY SIGN-IN – GROUP CERTIFICATE COURSE
### If you want to receive credit, please fill out the information below:

The month is_____ The day of the month is _____ The year is_____ Signature _____

Meeting location_____ Start time _____ Number of people in my Group _____

MY GROUP STUDIES ACCORDING TO THE GOGI CALENDAR (circle one)     YES     NO

## HOW TO USE – ULTIMATE FREEDOM

You can use the tool ULTIMATE FREEDOM at anytime. All you need to do is focus your attention on being of service and helping to make a situation better.

You use ULTIMATE FREEDOM by moving into a POSITIVE ACTION that helps someone else. When you practice this way of living long enough, you may find yourself beginning to live in ULTIMATE FREEDOM every day, and your life will be truly, forever, ultimately happy.

## TELL US WHAT YOU JUST READ

You have just finished reading the ULTIMATE FREEDOM Basics. The Basics consist of the weeks you study ULTIMATE FREEDOM, the KEYWORDS, STATEMENT OF PURPOSE AND OWNERSHIP, OBJECTIVE, TOOL INTRO and HOW TO USE ULTIMATE FREEDOM. Remember ALL GOGI Tools were written *by* prisoners *for* prisoners.

*In your own words, explain the GOGI Tool ULTIMATE FREEDOM:*_____

_____

_____

_____

_____

_____

_____

_____

_____

_____

_____

_____

_____

_____

**DAILY SIGN-IN – GROUP CERTIFICATE COURSE**
If you want to receive credit, please fill out the information below:

The month is_____ The day of the month is _____ The year is_____ Signature _____
Meeting location_____ Start time _____ Number of people in my Group _____
MY GROUP STUDIES ACCORDING TO THE GOGI CALENDAR (circle one)    YES    NO

# ULTIMATE FREEDOM Meeting

GOGI weeks begin on Monday. ONLY hold this meeting in the following weeks: (check the week you are studying the ULTIMATE FREEDOM Tool.)

❑4th Week of March    ❑ 4th Week of June    ❑4th Week of September    ❑4th Week of December

## Call Your Meeting to Order

*To be read by a volunteer:*
We call this GOGI meeting to order. We are gathered here today as a GOGI community of like-minded individuals who CLAIM RESPONSIBILITY for our lives in our own unique ways. We include the GOGI TOOLS FOR POSITIVE DECISION-MAKING as a supplement to our existing or potential spiritual and social support systems. We believe that the GOGI Tools help us on our journey toward internal freedom regardless of any perceived differences among us. We realize the GOGI TOOLS FOR POSITIVE DECISION-MAKING are learned according to a calendar and they are simple tools that may enhance many other practices that promote our health and well-being. We acknowledge the GOGI Tools as positive decision-making tools to help us in our daily living.

## The GOGI Purpose

*To be read by a volunteer:*
The purpose of GOGI is to provide simple tools to anyone interested in making more positive decisions in their lives. We do this through sharing the GOGI Tools which are taught in many ways and formats including independent-study, small group study, as well as formal educational programming offering course credit provided by institutions or educational organizations. Our purpose is to offer these tools as a positive and prosocial culture, not as a program, even in instances where GOGI is studied in a program format. We study the GOGI Tools according to the GOGI Calendar so no one will ever be alone in their study of GOGI. The GOGI Tools are to be shared freely among all people and should not be withheld for any reason.

## Reading of Your Tools *(To be read by a volunteer:)*

## The GOGI TOOLS FOR POSITIVE DECISION-MAKING are:

| | |
|---|---|
| BOSS OF MY BRAIN | CLAIM RESPONSIBILITY |
| BELLY BREATHING | LET GO |
| FIVE SECOND LIGHTSWITCH | FOR–GIVE |
| POSITIVE THOUGHTS | WHAT IF |
| POSITIVE WORDS | REALITY CHECK |
| POSITIVE ACTIONS | ULTIMATE FREEDOM |

## DAILY SIGN-IN – GROUP CERTIFICATE COURSE
### If you want to receive credit, please fill out the information below:

The month is_____ The day of the month is _____ The year is_____ Signature _____

Meeting location_____ Start time _____ Number of people in my Group _____

**MY GROUP STUDIES ACCORDING TO THE GOGI CALENDAR (circle one)    YES    NO**

## This Week's Objective

*To be read by a volunteer:*

Your goal this week is to practice creating freedom in your life by doing good things, even when no one is looking. ULTIMATE FREEDOM is this week's tool. You can be the boss of your level of freedom when you practice ULTIMATE FREEDOM each day.

## Check in/Recap of Your Prior Week

A brief check in when group members share their progress with the tools.

## Your Group Discussion

Please have volunteers or preassigned group members read from any of the GOGI books. This can be anything from any of the GOGI books related to the tool of this week (according to the GOGI Calendar). You may wish to have multiple people read from different GOGI books.

## Your Group Questions and Activities

This is a perfect time to have an activity. Your group can discuss this tool and, if completing GOGI as a program for credit, now is a great time to review or have your group members complete any required written assignments.

## Close Your Meeting

*We invite you to join us for our next meeting to be held (date) where we will study the GOGI Tool: _____ (refer to Calendar). If we are unable to hold next week's meeting we will refer to the Calendar for the tool we will study at the next meeting. Course credit is earned by meeting twelve to fifteen times, even if tools are skipped or repeated.*

## GOGI Pledge

*To be read by a volunteer:*

*May our commitment (group repeat)*
*To the study of GOGI (group repeat)*
*Grant us the joy (group repeat)*
*Of giving and receiving (group repeat)*
*So that our inner freedom (group repeat)*
*May be of maximum service (group repeat)*
*To those we love (group repeat)*
*And infinite others (group repeat)*

*This art is a gift to GOGI from Soliz.*

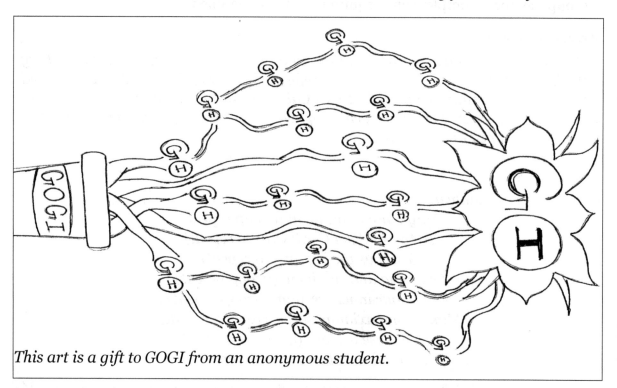

*This art is a gift to GOGI from an anonymous student.*

## DAILY SIGN-IN – GROUP CERTIFICATE COURSE
### If you want to receive credit, please fill out the information below:

The month is_____ The day of the month is _____The year is_____ Signature _____

Meeting location_____ Start time _____ Number of people in my Group _____

**MY GROUP STUDIES ACCORDING TO THE GOGI CALENDAR (circle one)     YES     NO**

## Weekly Course Worksheet ULTIMATE FREEDOM

*The word 'freedom' has many different meanings. You can be a free person physically, but still feel locked up emotionally. When you read about the tool ULTIMATE FREEDOM, what do you imagine?* _____

_____

*How is physical freedom from internal freedom?*_____

_____

_____

*There are many ways to do good and to be of service to others. In doing good deeds you will increase your internal freedom. What could you do this week to feel ULTIMATE FREEDOM?  I could:*

1. _____

2. _____

3. _____

*Most GOGI leaders agree that ULTIMATE FREEDOM is about serving others and doing good things.*

*How will you serve others? What good things can you do now and in the future?*

*Today I can...* _____

*Next week I can...* _____

*Next year I can...*_____

_____

*In just three words, describe your ULTIMATE FREEDOM:*

1. _____

2. _____

3. _____

*This art is a gift to GOGI*
*by GOGI Girl Jennifer B.*

## DAILY SIGN-IN – GROUP CERTIFICATE COURSE
### If you want to receive credit, please fill out the information below:

The month is_____ The day of the month is _____ The year is_____ Signature _____

Meeting location_____ Start time _____ Number of people in my Group _____

MY GROUP STUDIES ACCORDING TO THE GOGI CALENDAR (circle one)    YES    NO

## My GOGI Group Reflections

*In my GOGI Group this week I learned about the tool:* _____

_____

*This tool belongs to the section of tools called: The Tools of* _____

*I learned that this GOGI Tool has KEYWORDS. The KEYWORDS for this tool are:*

_____

_____

_____

_____

*If I choose, I could apply this GOGI Tool to my daily life. Below is an example of how this tool might help me make better decisions:*_____

_____

_____

_____

*What I liked most about my GOGI Group this week was:* _____

_____

_____

*Meeting in a GOGI Group is helpful to my learning and growth because:* _____

_____

_____

*Here are some things I want to write down so that I do not forget them in the future. They are my thoughts and my observations about life and GOGI.* _____

_____

_____

_____

KNOW YOUR GOGI

Positive Words.
Boss of My Brain.
Positive Thoughts.
Choice.
Let GO.
Tools of The Body.
Five Second Lightswitch.
Tools of Creation.
Claim Responsibility.
Tools of Moving Forward.
What IF.
Forgive.
Belly Breathing.
Positive Actions.
Reality Check.
Ultimate Freedom.
Tools of

Dustin Jeffries '16

GOGI

# RECAP & REVIEW

# GOGI

## WHAT YOU'VE LEARNED

# CELEBRATE AND REVIEW WHAT YOU'VE LEARNED

**DAILY SIGN-IN – GROUP CERTIFICATE COURSE**
If you want to receive credit, please fill out the information below:

The month is_____ The day of the month is _____The year is_____ Signature _____
Meeting location_____ Start time _____ Number of people in my Group _____
MY GROUP STUDIES ACCORDING TO THE GOGI CALENDAR (circle one)    YES    NO

# COMPLETION CELEBRATION
## AND OPEN BOOK QUIZ Meeting

## Call Your Meeting to Order:

*To be read by a volunteer:*
We call this GOGI meeting to order. We are gathered here today as a GOGI community of like-minded individuals who CLAIM RESPONSIBILITY for our lives in our own unique ways. We include the GOGI TOOLS FOR POSITIVE DECISION-MAKING as a supplement to our existing or potential spiritual and social support systems. We believe that the GOGI Tools help us on our journey toward internal freedom regardless of any perceived differences among us. We realize the GOGI TOOLS FOR POSITIVE DECISION-MAKING are learned according to a calendar and they are simple tools that may enhance many other practices that promote our health and well-being. We acknowledge the GOGI Tools as positive decision-making tools to help us in our daily living.

## The GOGI Purpose

*To be read by a volunteer:*
The purpose of GOGI is to provide simple tools to anyone interested in making more positive decisions in their lives. We do this through sharing the GOGI Tools which are taught in many ways and formats including independent-study, small group study, as well as formal educational programming offering course credit provided by institutions or educational organizations. Our purpose is to offer these tools as a positive and prosocial culture, not as a program, even in instances where GOGI is studied in a program format. We study the GOGI Tools according to the GOGI Calendar so no one will ever be alone in their study of GOGI. The GOGI Tools are to be shared freely among all people and should not be withheld for any reason.

## This Week's Objective

*To be read by a volunteer:*
Our objective has been learning the GOGI TOOLS FOR POSITIVE DECISION-MAKING to improve our lives and the lives of others by giving back. During this meeting, we will discuss what we have learned and take the open book quiz.

*This art is a gift to GOGI from Davida.*

# Open Book Quiz

**You may do this quiz as a group or individually. You may use any GOGI book to find answers.**

*What are the FOUR SECTIONS OF GOGI TOOLS that prisoners created?*

1. _____

2. _____

3. _____

4. _____

*What are the names of each of the GOGI TOOLS FOR POSITIVE DECISION-MAKING that prisoners created?*

1. _____

2. _____

3. _____

4. _____

5. _____

6. _____

7. _____

8. _____

9. _____

10. _____

11. _____

12. _____

## DAILY SIGN-IN – GROUP CERTIFICATE COURSE
### If you want to receive credit, please fill out the information below:

The month is_____ The day of the month is _____ The year is_____ Signature _____

Meeting location_____ Start time _____ Number of people in my Group _____

**MY GROUP STUDIES ACCORDING TO THE GOGI CALENDAR (circle one)     YES     NO**

What is the GOGI CALENDAR? Why do all students study the same tool at the same time? _____

_____

_____

Why do you think prisoners asked that GOGI have an OFFICIAL MEETING FORMAT? _____

_____

_____

In your opinion, why did prisoners create the GOGI Pledge? _____

_____

Can you write the Pledge from memory? If so, great! You are very GOGI! If not, find the Pledge in this workbook and write the GOGI Pledge below.

_____

_____

_____

_____

Does the GOGI meeting format remind you of any other meetings you have attended? _____

How? _____

What is your favorite day of the year? _____

What is the GOGI Tool studied in that week?_____

On what day were you born? _____

What is the GOGI Tool studied in that week? _____

Who created GOGI? And why do you think learning GOGI is so helpful to so many people? _____

_____

## DAILY SIGN-IN – GROUP CERTIFICATE COURSE
**If you want to receive credit, please fill out the information below:**

The month is_____ The day of the month is _____The year is_____ Signature _____

Meeting location_____ Start time _____ Number of people in my Group _____

**MY GROUP STUDIES ACCORDING TO THE GOGI CALENDAR (circle one)    YES    NO**

*While most GOGI students across the USA do not earn credits for the group studies, did you know that anyone may hold a GOGI meeting? There are tens of thousands of prisoners holding GOGI meetings in prisons globally, and they study according to the GOGI Calendar. Why does GOGI encourage all meetings to be 'on calendar?'* _____

_____

*Why does GOGI suggest meetings to and for anyone?* _____

_____

_____

*When you think of GOGI students in other countries and you imagine them working on the same tool that you study, at the same time, does it help you to think of GOGI more as a CULTURE and a WAY to live rather than an old fashioned "prison program?"*_____

*What does " GOGI Culture" mean to you?*_____

_____

*How can a "GOGI Culture" help prisoners?*_____

_____

*How can a "GOGI Culture" help prison officers?* _____

_____

*GOGI is offered in a "prison program" format, but GOGI is not limited to a program. What does this mean to you?*_____

_____

_____

_____

_____

_____

_____

## DAILY SIGN-IN – GROUP CERTIFICATE COURSE
### If you want to receive credit, please fill out the information below:

The month is_____ The day of the month is _____ The year is_____ Signature _____
Meeting location_____ Start time _____ Number of people in my Group _____
**MY GROUP STUDIES ACCORDING TO THE GOGI CALENDAR (circle one)     YES     NO**

*My favorite tool is:* _____ *I like this tool because:* _____

_____

*Here is how I can us this tool:* _____

_____

_____

*If I had the GOGI tools in the past, how may my life have been different?  I would have...*

_____

_____

*Having this tool now, here is what I have noticed about myself:* _____

_____

_____

*The biggest difference this tool can make in my life is:* _____

_____

_____

*Here is how I will explain the value of one of the The GOGI Tools to the first group that I mentor through the GOGI course.*

*The tool is:* _____

*I chose it because:* _____

_____

_____

*This is how I would explain it:* _____

_____

_____

_____

# *Congratulations GOGI Student!*

Dear GOGI Student,

In completing this cycle of GOGI studies, you have had the opportunity to learn simple tools for positive decision-making with a group of peers. Together, you have grown on your GOGI journey. In this course, GOGI has been offered to you in a program format. But, make no mistake, GOGI is not a simply a program. GOGI is actually more of a CULTURE and a WAY of living than it is a program with an end date. GOGI never ends.

GOGI is most often learned in a program format because programs provide an outline and a simple learning process. Programs permit measurement and a simple way to document the level of learning. Programs also make it easier to reinforce learning through repetition. In learning GOGI through the Group format, you've had the opportunity to integrate learning into your daily communication. The goal of this course has been to help you build new relationships, focused on positive decision-making, that last long after your course completion.

Completion of a course is a rare and wonderful accomplishment. Many individuals do not complete courses designed to teach positive decision-making, but you have achieved this wonderful honor. Congratulations. May I also invite you to repeat this course again and again. To truly build a skill, repetition is required. To build a culture, it is important that a new way of living is repeated often enough to become the new standard for a majority of individuals. When you and your friends repeat GOGI studies often enough, you have the power to shift the outcome of daily living for many people around you.

United with your peers, you can return to your communities as the SOLUTION to the problems that plague our neighborhoods. When you are relentless in your determination to live every single day with your GOGI Tools, you will find that others use those tools in their decision-making as well. Through your example of positive decision-making, and choosing to live your life The GOGI Way, you offer a solution to what was once perceived as an unsolvable problem.

In truth, there are no problems we can't fix when a sufficient number of community members choose to inspire the positive decisions of others through their own example. Ask yourself, are you prepared to BE that inspiration? Will you make the strong decision to be part of the solution? Are you an unwavering force for good, and an example of positive change?

Be honest with yourself, are you prepared to be the kind of neighbor people want living next to them?

Please continue with your study of GOGI. Continue to repeat cycles of GOGI often enough that your positive changes define you. Living as an example of positive change will declare to your community the type of individual you have decided to become. Remember, your ULTIMATE FREEDOM is dependent upon your willingness to live your life beyond your own wants, and your dedication to helping others.

GOGI-4-Life!

With Love,

Coach Taylor, Lead Volunteer

# GIFTS TO
# GOGI
# WEEK

This week, as a **GOGI** group you are to collectively create **GIFTS TO GOGI**. This can be a newsletter with everyone contributing, letters to donors, or letters to youth. It can also be letters to your Warden, Superintendent, sponsor, volunteers or state officials.

This week, week 15, is your opportunity to model service to others.

GOGI relies on input from students to direct our growth. On the following pages you have an opportunity to let your voice be heard. Please gently tear out and send us any pages you wish to share with us from the following section.

Send to: GOGI Education PO Box 2274 Mesquite, NV, USA 89024

# Our Gift to GOGI – our art, letter, poem, or activity

Our Group Name_____ Institution_____

Date _____

TEAR HERE AND MAIL TO GOGI

# Our Gift to GOGI – our art, letter, poem, or activity

Our Group Name_____ Institution_____

Date _____

# My Gift to GOGI – my art, poem, or activity

My signature_____ ID number _____Location _____

Print your name_____

# Our Gift to GOGI – our art, letter, poem, or activity

Our Group Name_____ Institution_____

Date _____

# My Gift to GOGI – my art, letter, poem, or activity

My signature_____ ID number _____Location _____

Print your name_____

# Your Opinion Matters!
# Your Suggestions and Impressions of GOGI

Today's Date: _____

My last name:_____ My first name: _____

My ID number:_____ My housing: _____

Institution _____

*What would make GOGI a stronger option for anyone seeking change?* _____

_____

_____

_____

_____

_____

_____

_____

*Our goal is 250,000 GOGI students in all prisons around the world. How might we reach this goal?*

_____

_____

*GOGI exists to develop positive community leaders. Did you observe this occurring in your GOGI group?* _____

_____

_____

**Write any additional comments on the back.**

## Your opinion matters! Send this to GOGI!

CPSIA information can be obtained
at www.ICGtesting.com
Printed in the USA
FFHW012010040619
52832420-58369FF

9 780997 287561